Studies in Continental Thought

EDITOR
JOHN SALLIS

CONSULTING EDITORS

Robert Bernasconi       James Risser
John D. Caputo          Dennis J. Schmidt
David Carr              Calvin O. Schrag
Edward S. Casey         Charles E. Scott
David Farrell Krell     Daniela Vallega-Neu
Lenore Langsdorf        David Wood

Martin Heidegger

# The History of Beyng

1. The History of Beyng (1938–40)

2. Κοινόν
Out of the History of Beyng (1939–40)

Translated by
**William McNeill**
and
**Jeffrey Powell**

Indiana University Press
Bloomington and Indianapolis

*This book is a publication of*

Indiana University Press
Office of Scholarly Publishing
Herman B Wells Library 350
1320 East 10th Street
Bloomington, Indiana 47405 USA

iupress.indiana.edu

Published in German as Martin Heidegger *Gesamtausgabe Band 69: Die Geschichte des Seyns: 1. Die Geschichte des Seyns (1938/40); 2. Κοινόν. Aus der Geschichte des Seyns (1939/40)* ed. Peter Trawny
© 1998 and 2012 by Vittorio Klostermann GmbH, Frankfurt am Main

English Translation © 2015 by Indiana University Press

All rights reserved
No part of this book may be reproduced or utilized in any form or by any means, electronic or mechanical, including photocopying and recording, or by any information storage and retrieval system, without permission in writing from the publisher. The Association of American University Presses' Resolution on Permissions constitutes the only exception to this prohibition.
The paper used in this publication meets the minimum requirements of the American National Standard for Information Sciences—Permanence of Paper for Printed Library Materials, ANSI Z39.48-1992.

*Manufactured in the United States of America*

Library of Congress Cataloging-in-Publication Data

Names: Heidegger, Martin, 1889–1976. | Heidegger, Martin, 1889–1976. Koinon. English.
Title: The history of Beyng / Martin Heidegger; translated by William McNeill and Jeffrey Powell.
Other titles: Geschichte des Seyns. English
Description: Bloomington: Indiana University Press, 2015. | Series: Studies in Continental thought | Includes bibliographical references.
Identifiers: LCCN 2015029162 | ISBN 9780253018144 (cloth : alk. paper) | ISBN 9780253018199 (ebook)
Subjects: LCSH: Philosophy.
Classification: LCC B3279.H45 G4713 2015 | DDC 193—dc23 LC record available at http://lccn.loc.gov/2015029162

1 2 3 4 5   21 20 19 18 17 16

# CONTENTS

Translators' Introduction — xiii

## THE HISTORY OF BEYNG (1938–40)

### THE HISTORY OF BEYNG. PART I

#### I. The History of Beyng

1. "The History of Beyng" Is the Name . . . — 5
2. The History of Beyng — 5
3. Western Philosophy — 6
4. The Truth of Beyng — 7
5. Are We? — 8
6. "We Are" — 8
7. Da-sein — 8
8. Beyng — 9
9. ἀλήθεια and Beyng — 9
10. That Truth . . . — 9

#### II. Contra-diction and Refutation

11. Contra-diction and Refutation (Re-iteration) — 13
12. The Historicism of Modernity and the History of Beyng — 15

#### III. Passage. The History of Beyng

13. The Consummation of Metaphysics — 19
14. Strife — 19
15. Strife — 19
16. World-relation — 19
17. The Historical Moment — 20
18. The Other Sovereignty — 20
19. What Is That? — 21
20. Beyng and Beings — 21
21. The Commencement — 21
22. What the Singular Need Is — 22
23. The History of Beyng — 23
24. The Representedness of Beings as the Actual — 23
25. Beingness as Representedness — 24
26. The History of Beyng — 24

27. Beyng as Sustainment — 25
28. The History of Beyng — 25
29. The History "of" Beyng — 26
30. The Failure to Recognize the Commencement — 26
31. The History of Beyng — 27
32. Magnanimity and Forbearance toward What Is Most in Coming — 28

### IV. The Consummation of Metaphysics
### Being's Abandonment

33. The Consummation of Metaphysics — 33
34. The Overcoming of Metaphysics. The Transition — 33
35. Being's Abandonment — 34
36. The End of the Modern Age in the History of Beyng — 34

### V. Τὸ Κοινόν

37. Passage — 39
38. Subjectivity and Being's Abandonment — 40
39. Κοινόν. On Passage — 40
40. On the Concept of Machination — 41
41. Machination (conceived in terms of the history of beyng) — 41
42. Machination and Devastation — 42
43. "Total" War — 44

### VI. The Sustainment. The Essence of Power
### The Necessary

44. "The Dis-tinction" — 47
45. The Trace Pointing to the Truth of Beyng — 47
46. The Trace Pointing to the Truth of Beyng. The Un-usual in the Essential Sense — 48
47. The Truth of Beyng — 48
48. Beyng — 48
49. The Decision. Beyng and the Human Being — 49
50. Decision — 50
51. Decision and the Future — 51
52. Beyng — 52
53. Beyng — 53
54. Machination and Event — 53

| | |
|---|---|
| 55. The Singular Decision | 53 |
| 56. Whence Being as Power? | 54 |
| 57. The Essence of Power | 54 |
| 58. The Determination of the Essence of Power | 62 |
| 59. Power "Needs" Power (Violence) | 64 |
| 60. Power and Violence | 65 |
| 61. Power and Crime | 66 |
| 62. The Essence of Power and Subjugation | 67 |
| 63. "The Demonic Nature of Power" | 67 |
| 64. Power and Truth | 67 |
| 65. Power and Leveling | 69 |
| 66. Power and Wretchedness | 69 |
| 67. "Power" and "System" | 70 |
| 68. Power and Public | 71 |
| 69. The Inhabitual and the Unexpected | 71 |
| 70. The Necessary | 72 |
| 71. Beyng-Historical Thinking | 73 |
| 72. The Essence of Philosophy | 74 |
| 73. The Human Being and Da-sein | 75 |

### VII. The Essence of History. "Commencement." "Beyng"

| | |
|---|---|
| 74. History | 79 |
| 75. History | 79 |
| 76. History | 79 |
| 77. The Essence of History | 80 |
| 78. History (Past and Having-been) | 81 |
| 79. The History of Beyng | 81 |
| 80. History and Beyng | 82 |
| 81. Concerning the Essence of History | 82 |
| 82. Commencement—History—The Suddenness of the Commencement | 83 |
| 83. Essence of History | 83 |
| 84. "Life" and "History" | 84 |
| 85. Historiography | 84 |
| 86. History | 85 |
| 87. History | 85 |
| 88. The Essence of History | 86 |

## VIII. Beyng and the Last God

| | |
|---|---|
| 89. The Last God | 89 |
| 90. The Countering | 89 |
| 91. Confidence and Dasein | 89 |
| 92. Beyng Is . . . | 90 |
| 93. Event | 91 |
| 94. Earth and World | 91 |
| 95. Beyng | 92 |
| 96. Beyng | 92 |
| 97. Beyng and the Nothing | 92 |
| 98. Beyng. Coming to Be Appropriated into the In-between | 93 |
| 99. Poverty | 93 |
| 100. Poverty | 94 |

## IX. Essence of History

| | |
|---|---|
| 101. The Beyng-Historical Concept | 97 |
| 102. Beyng | 97 |
| 103. The History of Beyng | 97 |
| 104. History of Beyng | 99 |
| 105. Bestowal and Reflection | 100 |
| 106. The Joint Crumbling of the German and Russian Worlds through Machination | 100 |

## X. The Owned

| | |
|---|---|
| 107. Bestowal and Impoverishment | 105 |
| 108. The Owned (Beings in Beyng as Event) | 105 |
| 109. The Owned | 106 |
| 110. The Owned | 106 |
| 111. Beyng | 106 |
| 112. The Owned | 107 |

### The History of Beyng. Part II

## XI. The Configuration of Saying

| | |
|---|---|
| 113. Beyng | 113 |
| 114. The History of Beyng | 113 |
| 115. The History of Beyng | 114 |

| 116. The History of Beyng | 116 |
| 117. The History of Beyng | 117 |
| 118. Beyng | 117 |
| 119. Beyng | 119 |
| 120. Beyng | 120 |
| 121. Guiding Words | 120 |
| 122. Only Beyng Is | 120 |
| 123. Beyng | 121 |
| 124. Beyng | 121 |
| 125. Beyng Is the Once | 121 |
| 126. Event | 122 |
| 127. The Event of Appropriation and the History of Beyng | 122 |
| 128. In the Event of Appropriation | 123 |
| 129. Truth as the Clearing | 123 |
| 130. Truth | 123 |
| 131. Concealing | 124 |
| 132. Truth | 124 |
| 133. Is Beyng Always? | 124 |
| 134. Beyng as Event of Appropriation | 125 |

## XII. The History of Beyng (Da-sein)

| 135. Da-sein | 129 |
| 136. That the Historical Human Being Comes into His Essence (Da-sein) | 129 |
| 137. Da-sein | 129 |
| 138. Protection | 129 |
| 139. Errancy | 129 |
| 140. Da-sein | 130 |
| 141. Being's Abandonment | 130 |
| 142. The Projections of the Being of Beings from Out of the Casting of Being Itself | 131 |
| 143. Seeking More Essentially the Other Commencement | 131 |
| 144. Word and Language | 132 |
| 145. The Decision | 132 |
| 146. Beyng | 133 |
| 147. The History of Beyng | 133 |
| 148. The History of the Human in Being | 133 |

149. History    133
150. Democritus, Fragment 269    134
151. The Thinker    134
152. They Rail Surreptitiously and Openly ...    134
153. History, Commencement, Downgoing    135
154. "Ego" and "Subject"    135
155. The Being of Beings and Beyngs of Beyng    135
156. The History of Beyng    135
157. Experience and Steadfast Insistence    135
158. The Leap Off    136
159. The First Commencement    136
160. The Essencing of Truth as Clearing of Beyng    137
161. The Human Being and Anthropology    137
162. The Human—*animal rationale*    138
163. Metaphysics—Anthropology    138
164. The First Commencement and the Human as ζῷον λόγον ἔχον    138
165. The History of Essential Thinking    139
166. Truth and Beyng. The Essence of History    139

### XIII. Beyng-Historical Thinking

167. Beyng-Historical Thinking and Philosophy    143
168. Beyng-Historical Thinking    143
169. "Philosophy" in the Other Commencement    143
170. "Philosophy"    144
171. The Commencement    145
172. Essential Thinking    145
173. Beyng-Historical Thinking    145
174. Freedom    145
175. Honoring and Valuing    146
176. Questioning    146
177. Pure Finding    146
178. The Sequence of Publications (in short treatises)    146

### Κοινόν
#### Out of the History of Beyng (1939–40)

Κοινόν. Out of the History of Beyng    151
Draft for Κοινόν. On the History of Beyng    169

Contents

## Appendix

Additional Materials for *The History of Beyng (1938–40)* 183
Additional Materials for *Κοινόν. Out of the History of Beyng (1939–40)* 188

Editor's Epilogue 189
German–English Glossary 193
English–German Glossary 201

Translators' Introduction

The present text offers a translation of Martin Heidegger's reflections *Die Geschichte des Seyns,* composed during the period 1938–40, and of the treatise Κοινόν. *Out of the History of Beyng,* which dates from 1939 to 1940. Together these are published under the title *Die Geschichte des Seyns* as volume 69 of the *Gesamtausgabe,* the "Complete Edition" of Heidegger's works. The German edition first appeared in 1998, with a second, revised edition, published in 2012. The present translation was prepared on the basis of the 1998 edition and subsequently revised to incorporate several corrections in the second edition and one correction for a projected third edition.

With regard to its philosophical significance, *The History of Beyng* belongs to a series of reflections dating from the mid- to late 1930s that begin with the *Beiträge zur Philosophie (Vom Ereignis)* (1936–38) and are continued in *Besinnung* (1938–39). All of these reflections, which have an exploratory and often tentative character, are concerned with thinking "being" (*Sein*) in a non-metaphysical sense as "event" (*Ereignis*). In each of these texts, Heidegger generally uses *Seyn,* an archaic spelling of *Sein,* to mark this understanding of being as event. Accordingly, we have used "beyng," an archaic spelling of "being," to render *Seyn* throughout the present translation. In addition to this endeavor to think "beyng" as event, the reflections contained in *The History of Beyng* are especially important for their meditations on the oblivion and abandonment of beyng intrinsic to beyng's history, for their remarks on politics and "race," and above all for their incisive critique of power, force, and violence. This critique of power, it may be recalled, arrives in the wake of Heidegger's monumental lecture courses on Nietzsche and the "will to power," lectures delivered during the years 1936–39. The treatise Κοινόν. *Out of the History of Beyng,* written during the period of the outbreak of World War II, comprises a reflection on the contemporary historical actuality from the perspective of the history of beyng and is notable for its analyses of "machination" (*Machenschaft*) as the configuring of power in the era of modernity and of communism as the culminating form of such machination.

On account of its exploratory and tentative character as a text in which Heidegger is in search of a language able to articulate a non-metaphysical thinking of beyng as event, the volume *The History of Beyng* is particularly resistant to translation. Several translation issues that run throughout the text deserve to be noted here at the outset:

*Austrag.* In ordinary German, the noun *Austrag* means a settlement or the resolution of a conflict; in Southern German usage, it can also refer to the part of an estate that a farmer passes on to his son. The related verb *austragen* has a range of meanings that include resolving or negotiating a conflict; delivering in the sense of handing over mail or goods; delivering in the sense of carrying a child through to full term; signing out (of a job); and taking out or erasing in the sense of removing an entry from a list. In Heidegger's usage, however, *Austrag* is another word for beyng as event; in the related text *Besinnung* (referred to above), Heidegger indicates that the word is not to be understood in terms of either settlement or removal but as the opening up or "clearing" of beyng as event: *"Austrag* does not mean settlement or removal, but rather opening up, clearing of the clearing—event of appropriation [*Er-eignis*] as *Austrag*—*Austrag* essential to the abyssal ground." *Austragen* literally means to bear or carry (*tragen*) out (*aus*), and in Heidegger's usage it seems to convey the sense of an extended carrying through and sustaining (as in carrying a child through to term). We have thus ventured to translate *Austrag* as "sustainment"; *austragen* as "to sustain"; and, where Heidegger hyphenates *Aus-trag*, we have rendered this as the "carrying out of sustainment."

*Ereignis* and related terms. Heidegger in this text deploys an entire range of terms related to *Ereignis* and built around the root *eigen,* "own." These include *Ereignung, Enteignung, ereignishaft, eigen, das Eigene, eigens, eigentlich, sich ereignen, Eigentum, eigentümlich, eignen, übereignen,* and *zueignen.* Our translations of these terms are indicated in the German–English Glossary at the end of this volume. In addition, however, Heidegger frequently hyphenates some of the cognates of *eigen,* and among such cases the hyphenation of the prefix *Er-* deserves particular mention. When Heidegger hyphenates *Er-eignis* and *Er-eignung*—as he does often throughout the text—this appears to emphasize not simply the bringing about or bringing into being of something (which the prefix often conveys in ordinary German usage) but especially the inaugural moment of the opening up or "event" of such bringing into being or letting something arise, of the emergence of something. At the same time, it draws attention to the *eigen,* to the appropriation or bringing something into its own. While we have generally translated *Ereignis* as "event" and *Er-eignis* as "event of appropriation," we have varied our translation of *Ereignung* and *Er-eignung* somewhat more, depending on context. Sometimes the emphasis seems to be on the inaugural moment, where we venture "opening of appropriation"; in other places, the emphasis seems to be more the "happening of appropriation" or "coming to be appropriated," and accordingly we have used these as variants. In general, our approach has been to convey a sense of the broader semantic playing field of these and other terms by way of variation that remains sensitive to context, rather than aiming for absolute consistency in the translation of particular words.

*Herr* and *Herrschaft*. These words have a broader and more flexible semantic range than any corresponding English word. *Herr* can mean "lord," "master," "sovereign," "one who rules"; *Herrschaft* can mean "lordship," "sovereignty," "rule," or "dominion." We have varied our translation of these and associated terms in accordance with context. See in particular sections 18 and 57 with regard to these concepts.

*Macht* and *Machen*. Two families of cognates that appear throughout the text are terms constructed around *machen*, "to make," and *Macht*, "power." Although they stem from different linguistic roots, they sound very similar and related; and in making the philosophical argument that all making is today subsumed under operations of power, Heidegger often weaves together in the same sentence words that stem from both lineages. This has the effect of emphasizing and intensifying the inextricable interwovenness of power and making, in the form of machination, within the epoch of modernity. Cognates of *machen* that appear in the text include *Machenschaft* ("machination"), *Machbarkeit* ("makeability"), *Machsamkeit* ("malleability"), *das Gemächte* ("contrivance"), *Gleichmachung* ("equalization"), and *die Mache* ("domain of making"). Among the more prominent cognates of *Macht* are *Bemächtigung* ("assumption of power"), *Entmachtung* ("disempowering"), *ermächtigen* and *Ermächtigung* ("to empower" and "empowering"), *Machtentfaltung* ("implementation of power"), *Machthaber* and *Machthaberschaft* ("possessor of power" and "possession or institution of power"), *mächtig* and *Mächtigkeit* ("powerful" and "powerfulness"), *Machtmehrung* ("increase in power"), *Machtträger* ("bearer of power"), *Machtverteilung* ("distribution of power"), *Ohnmacht* ("impotence"), and *Vormacht* ("dominant power" or "supremacy"). In addition, Heidegger invents the verbs *machten*, which we have rendered as "to power" or "to wreak power," and *übermachten*, "to overpower, to power over," and associated nouns *Durchmachtung* ("powering through") and *Übermächtigung* ("overpowering").

*Wesen, Wesung, Erwesung*. Heidegger generally uses *Wesen*, which normally means "essence," in the verbal sense of "essencing," and frequently writes *Wesung* to emphasize the latter. We have generally rendered *Wesen* as "essence" and *Wesung* as either "essencing" or "essential prevailing," depending on context. In addition, Heidegger coins the term *Erwesung* (sometimes hyphenated as *Er-wesung*), which—analogous to the *Er-* of *Er-eignung* discussed above—we take to be suggestive of "bringing about the essencing or essential prevailing" or, where hyphenated, of "opening the essencing or essential prevailing."

More context-specific issues of translation we have addressed in occasional footnotes; these are indicated by "Trans." Numbered footnotes indicate references internal or external to the text. Lowercase letters designate marginal remarks in either the manuscript (indicated by Ms.) or transcript (Trs.). For further details of the editing of the German volume, see the Editor's Epilogue.

We are grateful to Indiana University Press for the opportunity to undertake this extremely challenging translation. William McNeill thanks the College of Liberal Arts and Social Sciences at DePaul University for a summer research grant that facilitated considerable progress on this translation. Jeffrey Powell thanks the College of Liberal Arts at Marshall University for a faculty development award and the John Deaver Drinko Academy at Marshall University for providing additional time for work on the translation.

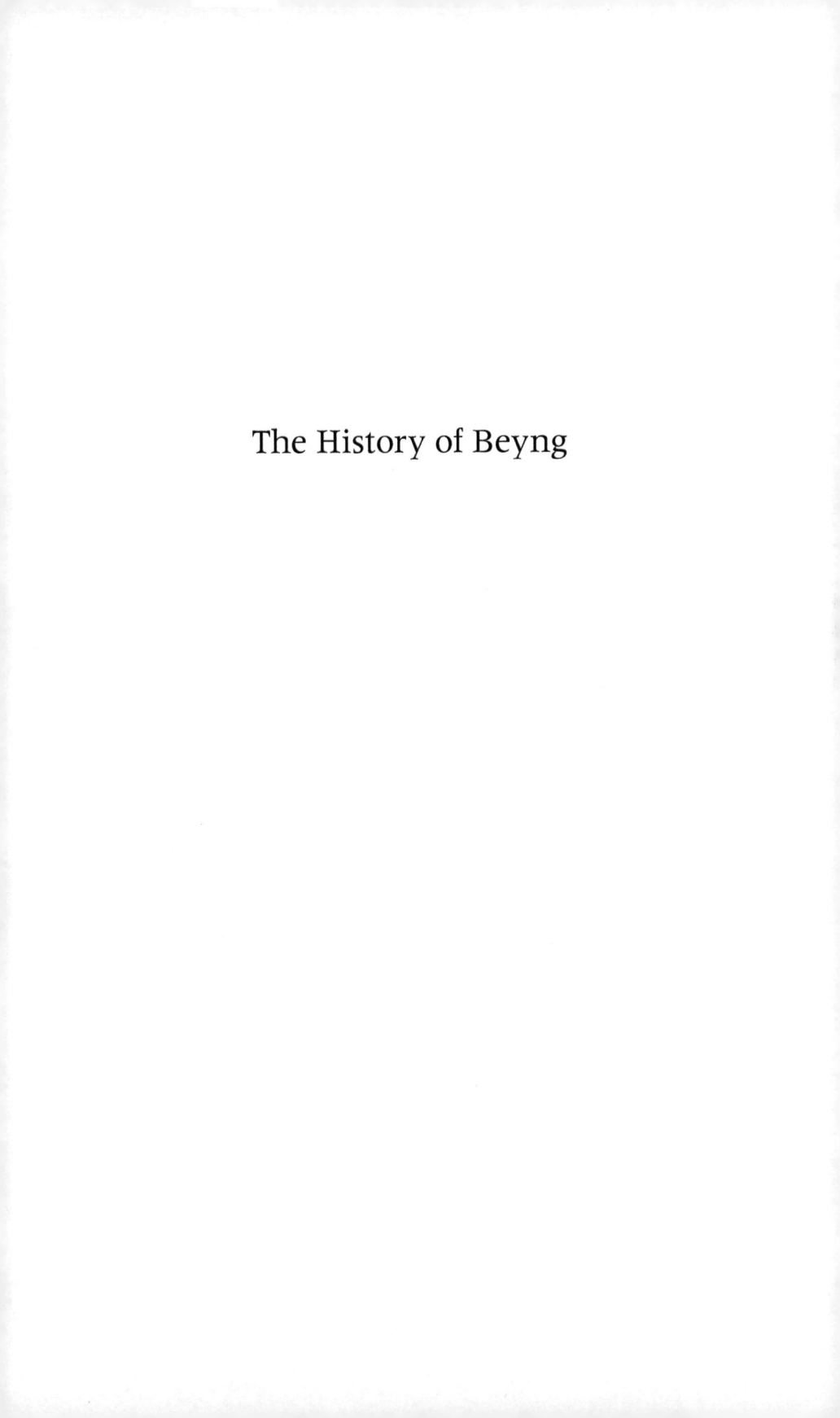

# The History of Beyng

# The History of Beyng
## (1938–40)

## The History of Beyng. Part I

# I. The History of Beyng

## 1. "The History of Beyng" Is the Name . . .

*"The History of Beyng"* is the name for the attempt to place the truth of beyng as event back into the word of thinking, and thereby to entrust it to an essential ground of historical human beings—to the word and its sayability. Whether the attempted saying itself belongs to the event and thereby participates in the stillness of that which *is* without having an effect or requiring an effectiveness can never be discerned by calculation. But the attempt would necessarily remain entirely outside of its realm, if it were not to know that it would more appropriately be named: *"To the very threshold."* And yet this hint once more diverts us away from the issue and toward the attempt to approach it.

The simple, mature conjoining of the *Contributions*[1] and *Mindfulness;*[2] the *Contributions* remain a framework, yet without structural articulation; *Mindfulness* is a middle, but not the source.

## 2. The History of Beyng

to be told only in the simple word, as told by the in-between which, transforming all relation to being, bears abyssally the sustainment in a way that humans are in general able to sustain within this inceptual realm.

World.
Earth.
Strife.
Humans.
God.
Countering.
Clearing.
Sustainment.
History.
Opening of appropriation.
Appropriative event.

---

1. *Beiträge zur Philosophie (Vom Ereignis)*. Gesamtausgabe vol. 65. Edited by F.-W. von Herrmann. Frankfurt am Main: Vittorio Klostermann, 1989. Translated as *Contributions to Philosophy (Of the Event)* by Richard Rojcewicz and Daniela Vallega-Neu. Bloomington: Indiana University Press, 2012.

2. *Besinnung*. Gesamtausgabe vol. 66. Edited by F.-W. von Herrmann. Frankfurt am Main: Vittorio Klostermann, 1997. Translated as *Mindfulness* by Parvis Emad and Thomas Kalary. New York: Continuum, 2006.

## 3. Western Philosophy[a]

Why is Western "philosophy" in its essence metaphysics?
Because in the *ground* of its essence it is "physics."
And to what extent, and why, is Western philosophy "physics"?
"Physics" here means knowledge (preservation of the truth) of φύσις. Φύσις is the determination of being found at the commencement,[3] and that therefore reigns throughout the entire history of Western philosophy.
Yet, being is that which philosophy thinks.
Yet why does physics come to be meta-physics?
What type of variation and entrenchment of physics is that?
Above all else: what does φύσις mean?
And *is* it the interpretation of the being of beings as a whole found at the commencement?
Is it even determinative for this interpretation?
And why?
Or is the why-question prohibited here, because it is profoundly inappropriate?
The history of beyng.
Is all this only the "philosophy of philosophy" and thus the degenerative outcome of an excess, which is the sign of an uprooting? Or, is something else imminent?
What speaks here is neither a "philosophy of philosophy" nor indeed a philosophy at all. Presumably, however, a readiness for philosophy enjoins its essence, a readiness that goes deep into its ground; and this is the grounding of a belonging to beyng. A rootedness opens up the path into the ground, an event propriated out of the refusal of beyng, neither fabricated nor thought up, yet thoughtfully attentive to the gentleness of the free, given over to the stillness that dwells supreme in the coming of that most in coming.
We appear to be inquiring about philosophy, yet in truth inquire only of beyng, for which philosophy remains the history of an essential belonging, one to which a thinker is from time to time admitted.

---

a. Trs.: *The Beyng-Historical Concept of the Western World* [*Abendland*]. The land [*Land*] of evening [*Abend*]. Evening consummation of a day of history (F.) and the transition to night; time of transition and preparation for morning. Night and day.

3. The term "commencement" translates the German *Anfang*. Where the adjective *anfänglich* or the gerund *anfangend* is used, we have generally rendered these as "inceptual" and "inceptive," respectively.—Trans.

Philosophy as something contrived does not lie within the sphere of this reflection.[4]

## 4. *The Truth of Beyng*

hitherto never yet recognized, even though it had to come to the fore within the open realm belonging to the commencement of Western philosophy itself, albeit not *as* the truth of beyng, and therefore it also never entered its questioning. Rather even its first, still entirely veiled apparition was henceforth buried—and yet it could not and cannot be eliminated.

Only from out of the need of beyng, however, can we first inquire after it.

Compare the interpretation of Aristotle's *Physics* B, 1 (first trimester 1940), p. 22ff.;[5] a hint of the truth of beyng proceeding from

---

4. The term "reflection" translates the German *Besinnung* throughout the present volume. *Besinnung*, however, does not carry the optical or reflexive connotation of reflection, such as one finds in German Idealism, and which Heidegger associates with the representational form of thinking that he criticizes. *Besinnung*, rather, implies a thoughtful or meditative pondering that follows the meaning or directional "sense" (*Sinn*) of something: in this context, the "essencing" of the truth of beyng, as Heidegger will indicate in §31 below. *Besinnung* is also the title of the 1938–39 text published as volume 66 of the Gesamtausgabe and translated under the title *Mindfulness* (see note 2 above for details). In his 1953 essay "*Wissenschaft und Besinnung*" (translated as "Science and Reflection"), Heidegger clarifies *Besinnung* as follows: "To follow a direction that is the way that something has, of itself, already taken, is called, in our language, *sinnan, sinnen* [to sense]. To venture after sense or meaning [*Sinn*] is the essence of reflecting [*Besinnen*]. This means more than a mere making conscious of something. We do not yet have reflection when we have only consciousness. Reflection is more. It is releasement [*Gelassenheit*] to what is worthy of question." See *Vorträge und Aufsätze*. Gesamtausgabe vol. 7. Edited by F.-W. von Herrmann. Frankfurt am Main: Vittorio Klostermann, 2000. Translated by William Lovitt in *The Question Concerning Technology and Other Essays*. New York: Harper & Row, 1977, 180 (translation modified). See also the translator's note in that essay concerning the meaning of *Besinnung* (155 note 1).—Trans.

5. First version in *Leitgedanken zur Entstehung der Metaphysik, der neuzeitlichen Wissenschaft und der modernen Technik*. Gesamtausgabe vol. 76. Edited by Claudius Strube. Frankfurt am Main: Vittorio Klostermann, 2009. Published version under the title "On the Essence and Concept of φύσις in Aristotle's *Physics* B, 1" in *Wegmarken*, Gesamtausgabe vol. 9. Edited by F.-W. von Herrmann. Frankfurt am Main: Vittorio Klostermann, 1976, 239–301. Translated as *Pathmarks*, edited by William McNeill. New York: Cambridge University Press, 1998, 183–230.

Parmenides' τὸ γὰρ αὐτὸ . . . ; cf. its revised interpretation from summer 1940.

### 5. Are We?

*Who* are we?
   Where are we?
   In what moment are we?
   Who are *we*?
   A configuration of questions in which *one* question arises—never with regard to "us," but "after" beyng. A disconcerting state of affairs in which beyng propriates.
   But *never* "dialectical," never as the play of opposites—entirely as propriative event, something singular.

### 6. "We Are"

*Who* are we?
   And indeed, *are* we?
   What does "being" mean? "Are" we, because and insofar as we come across ourselves, and do so in the *way* that we come across a tree or house? And do we come across ourselves in this way? And even if we do, do we thereby hit upon the way in which *we* are?
   Who decides about "being"?
   Or does being decide about every "who" and all questioning? And how does it do so? What is being? How should being be unveiled and be brought into its truth? What is truth?
   We stand in the most extreme region of these questions.

*

Propriation and the gentleness of supreme sovereignty, which does not require power or "struggle," but originary critical setting apart. Power-less holding sway.

### 7. Da-sein

Who could say it!
   The clearing of being. To *be* the *grounding* ground of this clearing.

This itself does not = being human, rather the latter as guardianship and founding.

*

The There [*Da*].
A trace of the There in the ἀλήθεια of φύσις.
But the trace has long since been extinguished—it can never simply be followed again, but must be found from one's own trail.

*

And what a jumble of misinterpretation the concept of Da-sein in *Being and Time* has assembled. Not least in Jaspers, the most desolate leveling-down. From where, then, can we still await an ear and an eye and—a heart?

## 8. Beyng

at its appointed hour will ward off human fabrication and take even the gods into its service, casting off the corruption of its ownmost essence—machination.

## 9. ἀλήθεια *and Beyng*

Because ἀλήθεια remained but a resonance, and ungrounded, even the question concerning the *clearing* already appears entirely disconcerting to us. The question of beyng can be unfolded solely from out of this question. Beyng thus remains still *more concealed* and *yet*— the turn!

## 10. That Truth . . .

That *truth*, in essence, is ungrounded and the human lays claim to truths without truth—will historical humankind ever comprehend this as the non-ground of all contemporary history?

II. Contra-diction and Refutation[1]

---
1. Cf. §21. The Commencement.

## 11. Contra-diction and Refutation (Re-iteration)

1. to what extent refutation impossible in genuine philosophy; im-possible, because not attaining the realm of truth belonging to philosophy at all, which always decides the *truth of being*.
2. in what sense the impossibility may *not* be interpreted:
    a) not as though it concerned the putative view once offered by an individual human being (an "I cannot do otherwise" on biological-historical grounds).
    b) not as though every "rational" discussion were impossible here and the "system" and standpoint were to be accepted or rejected.
    c) not as though the issue concerned the person of the thinker at all.
3. Rather, what is essential is the contra-*diction* (re-*iteration*):[2]
    a) this means a saying, fundamental assertion concerning being and its truth.
    b) this requires the most profound knowing and requires a guiding reflection, which admittedly can never be accomplished by way of mere exposition regarding right and wrong, but rather as a *questioning* leading toward and into a fundamental experience.
    c) accordingly, questioning in a manner never attained by a scientific "problem," because the latter precisely leaves unquestioned the *being* of beings (positivity of science).
    d) this questioning—the supreme freedom and binding in the sense of steadfast insistence within the truth of beyng.
4. The saying is re-iteration:
    a) in the double sense of the *against* and of inceptual renewal.
    b) the "against" does not concern an un-truth in the sense of incorrectness and untenability, but rather a true-ness that is *not sufficiently inceptual*.

---

2. Heidegger in this section plays on the similarity between the German words *wider* and *wieder*. *Wider* means against or counter to; *Widerspruch*, which Heidegger hyphenates to highlight the literal meaning, means contradiction, literally, a "saying against" (as in *der Satz vom Widerspruch*, the principle of contradiction—or of non-contradiction, as we would say in English). "Refutation" is in German *Widerlegung*, literally, a "laying against." *Wiederspruch*, by contrast, means a saying again, or re-iteration. In the present instance, Heidegger combines the two, *wider* and *wieder*, by inserting a parenthetical (e), writing *Wi(e)der-spruch*—thus implying both contra-*diction* and re-*iteration*, and with the emphasis on the *Spruch* or "saying."—Trans.

c) the "re-" says: that fundamentally it is always and ever the same thing that is thought, and that reciprocal irrefutability means not a sheer irreconcilability, but only an indication that it is always *the same thing* that is asked; which, however, simultaneously excludes any equalization and any diminution.
d) what is asked about—the truth of beyng—is what is most simple, this being what is most acute, which tolerates no diminution, such that the essential *unity* of thinkers consists precisely in their reciprocal irrefutability and separation.
e) to this belongs the deepest freedom, which is one with a steadfast insistence within the *history* of beyng.
f) for this reason, genuine contra-diction is not only that which is most simple, but as such, what is most seldom.
5. *Contra-diction is historical,* and for this reason its domain can never be attained historiographically, through acquaintance with an era and its affairs and views, but only from out of a questioning that seeks the truth of beyng. Cf. in this regard *Mindfulness,* §13, "Philosophy."[3]
6. On "refutation," and that means "science," cf. *Contributions,* §75, "Concerning the Meditation on Science"; and §76, "Propositions Concerning 'Science.'"[4] (Cf. also first trimester, 1940, "The Fundamental Concepts of Metaphysics,"[5] "Essence of Science," "Fundamental Concepts.")
7. Philosophy is not without grounds; yet its furnishing its grounds can never be the demonstration of some correctness, which necessarily has unquestioning recourse to an incommensurate truth concerning beings.

   Furnishing grounds is grounding in the sense of a knowing transposition into a knowing (steadfast insistence) that concerns the truth of beyng, and that means: a readying for coming to be appropriated through the event.
8. All philosophy hitherto, however, in the form of metaphysics gives rise to the appearance of a "science," especially in that it even names itself this and considers itself to be this, and repeatedly sets itself standards that make inadequate demands.

---

3. *Mindfulness.* Gesamtausgabe vol. 66.
4. *Contributions to Philosophy (Of the Event).* Gesamtausgabe vol. 65.
5. In: *Leitgedanken zur Entstehung der Metaphysik, der neuzeitlichen Wissenschaft und der modernen Technik.* Gesamtausgabe vol. 76.

And this is why an "effect" is expected of philosophy, one that it can never have. And that "effect" which is proper to it is not experienced in its abyssal character, or it is mischaracterized in a biological, psychological, or historiological manner.

Contradiction is not refutation, that is, not a presenting of, and giving grounds for, opposing statements about something objective, but rather fathoming the ground of an inceptual fundamental position within the truth of beyng and a steadfast insistence within it. Philosophy can never directly influence or alter beings—that which is actual—but it is capable of something more essential. It is, *if and when* it is, but this happens only seldom: a leap into the history of beyng, a leap that fathoms in a more inceptual manner the ground of the truth of beyng.

## 12. The Historicism of Modernity and the History of Beyng

*"Stances"* (another modern concept!) *that modernity makes possible and on occasion necessitates;* the freedom of the *subjectum*.

Meaning, stances toward a particular era in which a humankind and its generations live.

1. *One goes with the "times."* One wants to be with it, and to find oneself confirmed thereby. "Modernity"; one even *must* be with it. Here the "times," that is, the "present," are viewed differently each time (in their *seeds*, that is, in what is *newest—coming*)—in terms of the foreground or background.
   a) shallow progressiveness ⎫
   b) heroic realism              ⎬ = *new matter-of-factness*
                                  ⎭
2. One is constantly *against* the "times," insofar as one stands outside them, yet nevertheless uses them and casts them as opposition. Christendom, and in a historiological manner all "Renaissances."
3. A few leap ahead of the "times," not just into their "future" (that of the present), but into an essentially other history. The history of being. The "futural ones" in the *essential* sense.

# III. Passage
# The History of Beyng

## 13. The Consummation of Metaphysics

Nietzsche not only constitutes an end, that is, the need for another commencement, but this very need only necessitates that even in its consummation, metaphysics itself—and that means the *truth* of beings as a whole—must at the same time, if only in an entirely veiled manner, become essential and force decisions. And precisely this is what is understood with greatest difficulty by the end of this era. For on the one hand, it clings to a rejection of metaphysics by way of positivism, and on the other hand, the affirmation of metaphysics is so alien (cf. Κοινόν) that it becomes terrifying.

## 14. Strife

The earth is not a sector cut out of beings as a whole.
The world is not a sector cut out of beings as a whole.
Beings are not distributed between these two sectors.
Earth is essencing of beings as a whole.
World is essencing of beings as a whole.
Earth and world belong to the being of beings as a whole, and for this reason there is between them the strife that we are never able to think if we represent to ourselves a conflict or a contestation.
The strife itself must be comprehended from out of the crossing through of their countering, and both must be comprehended in terms of the event.

## 15. Strife

for supremacy—wherein? In bringing about the essencing of beyng.
Only in *strife* is that which looms forth bound into supremacy, *brought into its own.*
Everything earth, everything world, and neither the essence, and both the essencing.
Supremacy—from out of the event!

## 16. World-relation

World-relation. Admitted into the "earth." *Both* on account of *belonging to beyng,* and with beyng, *countering.*
Earth and life (that which loves) the darkening, towering-exceeding earthly drive. As *strife* to world.

## 17. The Historical Moment

1. What rules: power as dictatorship?
2. Where is the "event" and the "strength" for overcoming?
3. Does a signpost already point the way?
4. What does overcoming of "power" mean? Is it not the declaration of im-potence with regard to the actuality of the actual?
5. Being led astray by the prevailing "present":
   a) the disgruntlement of those who remain outside and those who come too late.
   b) the vanity of those who find confirmation as fellow travelers.
   c) the vacuity of those who take refuge in the past.
   d) the noise of those who go along with the present.

Everywhere reckoned in a merely "historiographical" manner and thought in terms of *subjectivity.* History not experienced.

*History* not the secular replacement for a disintegrated "eternity" (historiographical esteem, accomplishment, memory), *rather history as essencing of the truth of beyng.*

Inceptual historicity from out of beyng is that which comes toward us.

## 18. The Other Sovereignty[1]

Sovereignty over the essence of power.
   The annihilation of machination through the event of appropriation.
   The essence of sovereignty is changing. Yet why does "sovereignty" give the measure in general, and continue to do so even here?
   Being and beings. The origin of sovereignty lies in this "distinction," that is, it is within beyng itself.

\*

Whoever rules *over* power is sovereign.[a] A mere "yes" to power as the essence of actuality is the basest form of slavery.
   The one who transforms its essence is sovereign master of power. Such transformation springs from beyng alone.
   And *eventually* beings come before beyng and must fathom the ground and commencement of their truth in beyng and—reach into the abyss of ground.

---

1. Cf. foundational words: *sovereignty* [*Herrschaft*].
a. Ms.: Why, and in what way "sovereign."

## 19. What Is That?

What is that? Thrownness into the clearing? History.
What propriates and what is appropriated as *standing in the open?*
Steadfast insistence oriented toward a coming.
Forth, from out of *being as being, the in-between.*
Prevailing of the essence of truth: history.
The *distinction.*

## 20. Beyng and Beings

Beyng is never a "cause" for beings, insofar as by "cause" one means something that effects, which must always be of the nature of a being. *"Effect" in the sense of bringing forth and letting come forth* is taken from the *domain of beings.*

For the relationship of beyng and beings there is no correspondence in any domains whatsoever—this relationship is *singular and unique.*

And the unity of what is "distinguished" is the truth "of" beyng itself, into which beings on each occasion prevail in their "essence" as revealed.

## 21. The Commencement[2]

The commencement, which reigns over all that is to come, *is* only in commencing. That is to say: the commencement is the Same and in each case itself only so long as it goes back into itself, and thus preserves within itself that which it casts ahead, the truth of beyng, protecting itself against any reversal. Accordingly, a relationship to the commencement is only ever possible in such a way that the commencement is placed back into its own, into that protective preservation (of the essence of φύσις), and is respected in its singularity. Every other relationship is a turning away from the commencement, even if it awakens the semblance of being the opposite. In a turning away, the commencement is forgotten. The most insidious manner of forgetting is the progressive "repetition" of the same. One says the same with a constantly new indifference; the mode of saying and interpreting changes.

---

2. Heidegger in this section distinguishes between two senses of "the same": *das Selbe* and *das Gleiche.* "The same" in the sense of *das Selbe,* as the section makes clear, entails retrieval with difference; whereas "the same" in the sense of *das Gleiche* is the mere repetition of what is self-same or identical. We have here rendered *das Selbe* as "the Same" and *das Gleiche* as "the same."—Trans.

The "repetition" [*Wiederholung*] (iteration) of the same is fundamentally different from winning back a relationship to the *Same* that occurs in a retrieval or fetching back [*Wieder-Holung*]. What is the Same is retained when it is not adopted as the same, but rather is appropriated as that which is different and distinguished. The distinction emerges from the respective character of commencement with which the commencement commences in each case. The commencement, however, remains the same, that is, without commencement, whether it is acknowledged as a *preliminary stage* and thus "overcome," or whether it is apparently brushed aside by "radical overturnings" or renewed by "renaissances."

All "renaissances" only bring what is past into conformity with the times and precisely fail to leave it its own inceptual character. All "radical overturning" merely assumes as its overturning the already destroyed, no longer inceptive commencement. No "revolution" is "revolutionary" enough. In accordance with its essence, it remains a half-measure, for through its overturning it merely one-sidedly accentuates the other, already available side of what has gone before, at most intensifying it into the unconditional. Yet the entanglement thereby reaches its highest degree, and the characteristic sign of this is to make itself inaccessible to itself and to reject all reflection as being inappropriate. Everything "revolutionary" is merely the dependent counterpart of the "conservative." Both maintain themselves in what has gone before and is past, and institute it with a view to a perpetual today.

The inceptive relation to the first commencement, however, at all times stands *under* the first commencement, even when it, the other commencement, is more inceptual.

This "standing under" is what is astonishing about thrownness, which can be experienced only from out of the history of beyng and is to be taken on, in the manner of steadfast insistence, in Da-*sein*, in the grounding of the truth of being.

Da-*sein* and it alone is that which is thrown—exposed to the open realm of the primary projection of the first commencement.

Whoever withdraws from such thrownness is fettered out of the history of beyng and into the corrupted history of machination, and can there perform the servitude of his "freedom."

## 22. *What the Singular Need Is*

To disrupt history through the leap into the over-coming of metaphysics, and thereby to help to raise beings as a whole out of the hinges of machination.

A freeing into freedom for the truth of beyng.

*Such thinking is in-human* (does not turn to standards or goals or motivations belonging to humankind hitherto).
*Such thinking is god-less* (cannot appeal to a mission or mandate and rest content with that).
Such thinking is—Da-*sein*. The suddenness of the moment of another commencement of the history of beyng.
Steadfast insistence within this leap in is *first and foremost* more essential than every communication, instruction, or negotiation, as though what is at stake were a direct intervention to change human beings and things!

## 23. The History of Beyng

The reserved and ungrounded truth of beings as such (νοεῖν—εἶναι).
Being as οὐσία that has slipped away from φύσις.
Οὐσία as ἐνέργεια, *actus*, actuality.
Actuality as *representedness of effectiveness*.
Effectiveness and objectivity (objectification).
Objectification and being unleashed upon "beings" (object).
Dominant power of beings and being as effectiveness: power.
Power and machination.
Being unleashed upon beings and being's abandonment of beings.
Refusal as the concealed truth of being.
Refusal and resonance of coming to be appropriated into a belonging to the truth of beyng.
Coming to be appropriated as beyng itself: event.
The appropriative event as sustainment: the in-between.
In this history nothing gets lost—and at times it prevails more essentially in the simplicity of what has been.

## 24. The Representedness of Beings as the Actual[3]

This re-presentedness [*Vor-gestelltheit*] in the sense of a "certain," securing representing [*Vorstellen*], that is, provision of the actual as procured and effective.
Whence ἐνέργεια with Leibniz, while maintaining οὐσία, now also as *vis*, "force," neither "*possibility*" nor "*actuality*."

---

3. The German word used for "representation," *Vorstellen*, has the literal sense of setting (*stellen*) before (*vor*) oneself. In the present section, Heidegger sometimes hyphenates *Vor-stellen* and *Vor-gestelltheit* ("re-presentedness") to emphasize this aspect of representation. Where hyphenated, we have rendered *Vor-stellen* as "representational setting-before."—Trans.

Not the "between," either, but the *"origin"* and that which properly is, as *nisus, conatus.*
Possibility and actuality then also transformed accordingly.
*Nisus* and the *empowering of power.* "Urge."
What becomes of "nature"?
And what sense does the science of nature now receive?
*Mechanics* precisely sets free the forces.
Whence: living beings as "organism."
From organism to the "organic."
The organic and the elementary character of *drives.*
Drive and urge as what is "actual."

\*

Representedness not in the sense of the ἰδέα (the latter *not* to be taken *aesthetically-optically*)—φύσις.
Representedness just as little in the sense of an empty *purely naive* [?] *objectification.*
*Representational setting-before* as bringing before oneself the actual as that which is effective, and at the same time thereby setting loose upon that which *"is"* in such a way.
Setting before oneself in the ambiguity of *repraesentatio.*
*Representational setting-before* and *"technicity."*

### 25. Beingness as Representedness

means: objectification of the "actual" (of what has an effect) into effectiveness.
Technicity essentially belongs to such objectification as the essence of its truth.

### 26. The History of Beyng[4]

beyng
φύσις
ἰδέα
οὐσία
ἐνέργεια
*actus* (actuality)

---

4. Cf. §39. Κοινόν.

*perceptum* (re-presentedness) ⎫ subjectivity a.
*objectum* (objectivity) ⎭
actuality ⎫
(ἐνέργεια—*vis* primitiva activa, Leibniz) ⎬ subjectivity b.
will and reason (German Idealism) ⎭
power (Nietzsche's will to power)
machination
being's abandonment
refusal           coming     ↑
dis-appropriation           de-cision, "transition?"
eventful appropriation        ↓
event
sustainment
history

The telling of this history stands at once within the long-nurtured misinterpretation of being a reporting and proclaiming; whereas the word is "valid" only in that it *is* beyng-historical.

## 27. Beyng as Sustainment

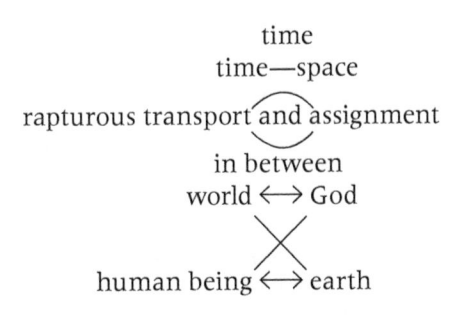

time
time—space
rapturous transport and assignment
in between
world ⟷ God
╳
human being ⟷ earth

Between and the transporting-assigning counter-turning.
The nature of counter-turning: strife/countering—*sustainment*.
Steadfast insistence and beyng.
"Willing" (?), that beyng may prevail in its essence.
    As we are steadfastly insistent, so are we appropriated into an enduring of the *strife* and of countering and of the *sustainment*.

## 28. The History of Beyng

First commencement: rising up, (idea), machination. ⎫ *Beyng*
Other commencement: event. ⎭

The transition is not between one commencement and another; at the commencement there is no transition of history. Every commencement is something sudden. All the longer and more concealing are preparation and what follows after and the transition into the sudden.

Sudden is the commencement in its initiation and breaking-off.

Only within *history* is the commencement appropriated eventfully as commencement—before that, suddenly, into what lies ready as the ahistorical of historiography. But already beyng as rising up. Only out of the other commencement—the first.

The history "of" beyng as the essential prevailing of beyng, within which, at the same time, history is revealed into its essence (and the corruption of its essence).

The history of beyng is abyssally different from all historiography concerning beings, but equally so from the "history" arrived at within such historiography by objectification.

The history of beyng is the prelude that prevails in its essence.

## 29. The History "of" Beyng[b]

The *overcoming* (passage over) of metaphysics. (Beingness). Machination (On *Mindfulness*).[5]

Appropriative event. (Beyng). Sustainment.

History. (Essential prevailing of truth).

The disappearance of the human being. (Da-sein). The throw toward of Da-*sein*.

The last god.

*The bestowal of impoverishment.*

The unfathomable stillness of the singularity of the simple, prevailing in its essence around the sustainment.

## 30. The Failure to Recognize the Commencement

You can make whole only from out of the whole. And the latter?

---

b. Ms.: *Simplest Configuring*. Letting unfold what was thought in the *Contributions* and *Mindfulness*.

Letting unfold from out of beyng as the truth of beyng to the beyng of truth as Da-sein.

5. *Mindfulness*. Gesamtausgabe vol. 66, §9. Machination.

Not furnishing what is lacking, therefore, the passion for reason, for instance, nor the converse, but each in themselves in each case, in their counter-play—out of the *origin!*
*How so, such an origin?*
Not *"inversion,"* either.
The failure to recognize the commencement is promoted most of all by the awakening of a semblance of originality along the lines of making whole or inverting what has gone before.

## 31. The History of Beyng

The list of names is only apparently a sequence of titles. It says all at once the simplicity of the appropriative event from φύσις to sustainment. A stranger—in errancy—is the human being within the history of beyng, and made a fool, moreover, by the historiography of beings.

The telling of the history of beyng cannot "secure" itself by a flight into what is customary, or what is worse—into altered forms of presentation that oppose what is customary.

This telling is also unable to cast off the semblance of the "fragmentary," whether one takes this to be the incompleteness of an accustomed and expected whole, or as its own intrinsic form of "expression" (for example, in the sense of the "aphorism" employed by Nietzsche).

The telling—incalculable like beyng itself—is *one* essential prevailing of its truth, in the manner of a keeping silent its sustainment.

The telling does not report on the course of a "history" in which events and their anchor points coalesce. The telling does not describe anything present at hand, does not narrate past events, and does not calculate in advance what is to come.

If we name this telling a "reflection" [*Besinnung*], then this refers to a transformation of humankind into its "senses" [*Sinn*], which here means, and means solely: the essential prevailing of the truth of beyng.

Transformation into that which the history of beyng hitherto did not permit, and henceforth can only beckon into a steadfast insistence within Da-sein—which Da-*sein* is the hitherto concealed ground of the grounding of the abyss of its sustainment.

The transformation, however, is undertaken not on account of the human being; rather, for the sake of beyng Da-sein prevails in its essence.

Thus the "reflection" always remains in danger of being taken as an "existentiell" "ethics" and the like, and of working against what the history of beyng holds in store for the future: the vanishing of the human being—of the *animal rationale* and of subjectivity.

The telling tells only insofar as it is tellingly history of beyng. For us, this means: insofar as the word steadfastly insists within the transition.

The telling is the telling of thinking, and in the other commencement, thinking is the preparation of poetizing.

Certainly, for its part the "reflection" has its essence with regard to the history of beyng thoroughly prescribed for it, and it therefore tells the essential tellings and the singular decision.

And yet, time and again it brushes with the danger of the historiographical: that thinking after all remains a concomitant inquiry seeking out beyng. Yet can this danger ever be eradicated from the midst of human endeavors? Never. But it will always be necessary to encounter it differently and more decisively in order to acknowledge it as an essential danger.

For this reason, thinking must think anew, fifty or a hundred times, the Same, and attempt to arrive at the place of the Same, until something simple once succeeds.

For this reason, every historiographical impetus must become ever more indifferent, until history alone propriates the word and the word then speaks beyng into beings, clearing the latter.

Yet how should thinking—which for two thousand years has been seeking beings and taking them to be what is real, and unquestioningly finding being in a "reality" that is supposedly unclarifiable and in need of no clarification—how should our previous thinking first be transformed into knowing of beyng, and to knowingly experience it as a coming?

Yet ask beyng, and in it the god responds as the word, that is to say: in the word "of" beyng, godship comes—countering humankind—with humankind to the strife of earth and world.

## 32. *Magnanimity and Forbearance toward What Is Most in Coming*

Nothing squandered on interests, ways of being saved, or "salvation."

The history to come has its commencement as history of *beyng* through the grounding of its truth. Mere change in the *human being* from Christian to pagan or back once again to Christian is incapable of bringing any history into the free. Equally impotent is the alteration of *beings*. Moreover, the alternative of Christian or pagan is still a Christian question, since there is paganism only when seen from a Christian perspective. The historical commencement stands outside of this alternative; it is not religious—yet for this reason alone it stands in an untarnished expectation, one that has no aspiration of securing human salvation.

The superior expectation that gives time and space.

The *renunciation* of "vital interests" and forms of "eternal bliss" as measures of beings and of busying oneself with them.

Renunciation—the courage of magnanimity and forbearance—renunciation, no turning away in despair, but the confidence of superior expectation from out of a knowing of beyng.

# IV. The Consummation of Metaphysics
## Being's Abandonment[1]

---

1. Cf. technicity.

## 33. The Consummation of Metaphysics

is characterized by being's oblivion, prevailing within it and lending it support, becoming *unconditional,* that is to say: beingness (misinterpreted as "idea") has not only gone up in smoke through the inversion of Platonism, but the beings that are now, for the first time, properly left over ("life") are posited as all there is and as the root of everything. Everything else is "expression" and "language of forms." An unrestricted lack of need comes to dominance, one that believes it can make do with beings themselves, since these are, after all, the element of plenitude. There is no need for "being," since it counts as what is "abstract."

To what extent does Hegel indirectly prepare and form part of this consummation of metaphysics?

The oblivion of being is the metaphysical installation and entrenchment of being's abandonment, which is necessarily completely concealed in this process.

Being's abandonment of beings consists in the exclusive priority of beings, of whatever happens to be at any given time in this era.

And the oblivion of being is testified to most clearly in the fact that in its belonging to these beings, in its certainty of belonging to them, it espies the sole and highest thing.

This certainty makes every question concerning truth superfluous and is itself interpreted as the supreme freedom.

For in turn—all that does not affirm beings, and beings alone, counts as *romanticism*—flight.

And so the oblivion of being thrives on its not understanding what it purportedly overcomes: Platonism and *its* ground.

## 34. The Overcoming of Metaphysics. The Transition

The transition out of metaphysics into questioning in terms of the history of beyng is in essence a passing over of metaphysics in the sense that it is no longer possible to question in the manner of metaphysics.

The overcoming does not arise from a "critique" of metaphysics but rather is the history of the necessity of grounding the truth of beyng from which questioning proceeds in an inceptual manner. In this regard there is no "transition" in the sense of a continual sliding over from metaphysics into a supposed suprametaphysics or absence of metaphysics: rather, the questioning is fundamentally different and within a historical reflection can certainly be pointed toward in a comparative manner, yet never accomplished in its own terms, which is the presupposition of the comparison.

## 35. Being's Abandonment

Being has abandoned beings: in each case this one and that one, in each case now and then, in each case there and here, the push is toward what is next within the domain of a makeability that is ascribed to beings. This ascription, however, is only a belated Yes to what it has already effected and enticed into busied activity. On each occasion, particular beings now offer themselves everywhere and constantly in their makeability. Beings depend upon their malleability, but without knowing or conceding such malleability as being. Beings abandoned by being—how, then, are they supposed to be abandoned?

Through the fact that they admit of no reflection upon being and its truth in the sense of a decision that would have to profoundly unsettle beings as a whole. Being's abandonment does not, therefore, mean unhitching beings from being: on the contrary, in such abandonment what is abandoned still remains related to that which abandons it—assigned to it—such that it depends upon that which abandons it, albeit in different ways. The abandonment is an essential one whenever that which abandons as such is no longer knowable, and yet a veiled semblance embraces everything.

This no longer admitting receives its own "stubbornness" and decisiveness from the fact that it has made a standing in truth un-necessary. The need has vanished because all beings have become explicable, and above all being too. One need only be acquainted with the constitution of the human being, and that everything is played out within the making that attends his fabrications. What is more illuminating, more convincing and elevating, and at the same time more endless, than such knowledge?

In the "light" of such knowledge the human being is blinded and sees only himself—"anthropology." This blinding, however, admits being, as the blindness of the oblivion of being.

## 36. The End of the Modern Age in the History of Beyng

The metaphysical event of the consummation of modernity is the empowering of "communism" as the historical constitution of the era of consummate meaninglessness [*Sinnlosigkeit*]. In keeping with the concept of meaning [*Sinn*] thought in *Being and Time*, this word refers to the projective realm for the projecting of being upon its truth. And "truth" signifies the revealing setting free of being into the cleared dimension of its essential presencing. Meaning-lessness, therefore, refers to truthlessness: the absence of the clearing of being.

As soon as this event occurs and "being" is nevertheless named as before, it assumes the role of the unquestionable and most general word for what is most general and vacuous, which extends to the unimaginable, most extreme limit of what can be represented. The being of beings, though constantly referred to in every comportment, saying, and silence of the human being, has renounced a clearing and determination of itself. This meaning-lessness attains its consummation through the absence of the truth of being itself sinking into unrecognizability, as soon as beings, which are named from being and after being, are abandoned by being. Beings, in what and how they are, and in that they are thus and thus in each case, are abandoned to the calculative planning and manipulative mastery of human beings, and humans are out to maintain themselves as those engaged with beings that can be made. ("Culture" and "technicity" in a modern-metaphysical sense, but such humankind already the essential consequence of the truthlessness of beyng.) *Being's abandonment* of beings has as its consequence the human being's establishing the securing of his essence in the thoroughgoing makeability of beings. Beyng abandons beings insofar as each respective being offers itself in its makeability and gives authoritative priority to what is human-made, a process, however, in which the human being fails to give thought to the makeability of beings in its essence and in the grounding of its essence, and in such a way, once again, that beings nevertheless remain admitted into the clearing of being, unrecognized and groundless as the malleability of everything. In such abandonment, that which has been abandoned is indeed not cut off from that which abandons, but rather assigned to it in such a way precisely that it still constantly "relies" upon it,[2] and does so even when what is abandoned forgets both that which abandons and its own abandonment. In an abandonment of beyng, beings, however, are released by beyng, because within the unseen light of the makeability of beings, only beings alone ever count, and "being" is demoted to a mere hollow word.

Yet this is an illusion, albeit one that is necessarily produced by being's abandonment. Even in being's abandonment of beings, beyng

---

2. The German *sich auf es "verläßt"* here more literally suggests "abandons" itself to it.—Trans.

still prevails in its essence.[a] For precisely in a time when meaninglessness is consummated and humankind is seduced into the boundless makings of the makeability of beings, as though it were the mastering of "being," then "values" ("values" of "life" and "culture") are proclaimed as the highest goals and forms of goal for the human being. "Values," however, are only the translation of being in its truthlessness into mere titles for what can have validity within the exclusive sphere of malleability, as what can be estimated and calculated. The emergence of the manifold variations of the "thought of value" in "worldviews" confirms that beings have been fully delivered over to being's abandonment. And the will to a "revaluation of all values," in no matter what direction it may be accomplished, accomplishes the final entanglement in consummate meaninglessness.

Yet to what extent is "communism" the historical configuration of the era of consummate meaninglessness? "Historical configuration" means that configuration of being that supports in advance the basis and the leeway for all decisions and modes of comportment of an era toward beings, thus to determine for this era the manner in which it belongs to "history." "History," however, is the way in which the truth of beyng is grounded and cultivated, confused and abandoned, passed over and forgotten. "Communism," however, in the midst of beings brings to dominance over beings that being which remains left over for beings through being's abandonment of beings.

---

a. Ms.: The loss and deprivation of beyng, the awakening in such loss, the refusal—their sign: the inhabitual.

# V. Τὸ Κοινόν[1]

---
1. Cf. III. Passage. The History of Beyng.

## 37. Passage

Being and objective actuality (modern metaphysics)
(Technicity)
Actuality and power
Power and communism
Communism and machination
Machination and devastation
Devastation and meaninglessness
Meaninglessness and being's abandonment
Being's abandonment and truthful safekeeping ("Ripe . . .")[2]

\*

Truthful safekeeping and refusal
Refusal and disappropriation
Disappropriation and appropriation
Appropriation and event
Event and sustainment

\*

Sustainment as beyng
Beyng and truth
Truth and Da-sein
Da-sein and history
History and de-cision
De-cision and beyng
Beyng and abyssal ground
Abyssal ground and the highest
The highest and the nearest

\*

Beyng and φύσις

Each the Same, and this Same in each case in turn what is most alien.
Commencements are always inceptual, without transition.
The unfathomable stillness of the uniqueness pertaining to the singularity of the simple.

---

2. Cf. Horror, *Mindfulness*. Gesamtausgabe vol. 66, §70. Gods. The Essential Knowing.

### 38. Subjectivity and Being's Abandonment

The *subjectivity* of humankind the distinctive securing of being's abandonment brought about through metaphysics.

The subjectivity of humankind characterizes modernity as such, because modernity itself is determined from out of the consummation of metaphysics; this *consummation*, however, consists in the empowering of the essence of being's power as machination.

The essential consequence of *subjectivity* is nationalism of the peoples and socialism of the people. In each instance a claim to power is asserted for the sake of power itself and therefore intensified and made more acute through such power itself in its essential exceeding.

The essential consequence of this history of subjectivity is an unconstrained struggle for the securing of power and therefore *unlimited wars* that take on the empowering of power. These wars are, in metaphysical terms, something *essentially* different from all previous wars.

The stages and forms of the power positions assumed by subjectivity in the individual nations and socialisms differ, and correspondingly differ from themselves in accordance with their war-like essence, and are veiled even in relation to themselves.

Subjectivity and *it alone* gives rise to the highest objectivity (in the form of technicity).

### 39. Κοινόν
### On Passage

No "*transition*" or "*passage across*" and no "*overcoming*"—all of this is still thought in counterplay to that which is contrived within machination. The devastation and being's abandonment and truthful safekeeping of beyng within itself as concealed sustainment is history of beyng (essencing of its truth).

"Transition" and "overcoming" are historiographical-technical terms, not from the history of beyng.

*

Here there are no attempts at the alteration of "worldviews" or transformation of "cultures."

That which is against a coming, in becoming set into the corrupted essence of machination, devastation, is thereby released by beyng itself from beyng, and abandoned to its meaning-lessness.

Yet this refusal of beyng can endure for a long time, and in running its temporal course it requires a steadfast insistence of its own within inceptive Da-sein. In terms of humankind this means: enduring our not belonging to it, avoiding the errancy of resistance, knowing the singular need.

*First our being equal to the devastation.* No flight into what has gone before, no leaping ahead into precipitously contrived "futures."

Enduring the devastation—in the inconspicuousness of our inability.

(Harder still is—to think the devastation as devastation for the first time in thinking ahead in an inceptual manner.)

Enduring the devastation. In its relinquishing of beings to being's abandonment, the refusal of beyng must strike within it, granted that the human being is capable of remaining within the temporal course of the history of being, and not stealing away backward or forward.

It remains difficult to tell which is more portentously fateful with regard to the endangering[a] of steadfast insistence: the flight into what has gone before, or the rush into the new, or mere "heroism" with a view to what is "presently" at hand, or salvation in the eternal.

## 40. On the Concept of Machination

If machination is determined, among other things, by calculation and the calculative, then this does not mean the obsession with "profit" or the seizing of advantages. Calculating is here the name for an essential transformation of λόγος, thus one determined in advance—the planning institution and accommodation of "interests," the erection of these as "supreme goals" that perhaps exclude all self-interest.

We can deny the lust for profit, and therefore after all in essence still affirm calculation before all else.

## 41. Machination (conceived in terms of the history of beyng)[3]

This word names that essence of being that decisively places all beings into makeability and malleability. Being means: being installed with a view to malleability, and in such a way that this malleability itself maintains such installation in the domain of making.

---

a. Ms.: *Everywhere historiography and technicity of beings!!*
3. Cf. *Mindfulness.* Gesamtausgabe vol. 66, §9. Machination.

In terms of the history of metaphysics, machination can be elucidated by *beingness* in the sense of being set before us or re-presented, with a view to being set forth or produced in whatever variation.

Machination, as the beingness of beings, is of the essence of beyng, its being cast away into the forgotten and ungrounded truth, that is, the unquestionable character of being and of the "is."

The word "machination" [*Machenschaft*], in terms of the history of its essence, here signifies a relation to φύσις, insofar as φύσις was at once regarded as a mode of ποίησις (of the domain of making) in the broadest sense.

The word means an essential prevailing of *being* and not, for instance, the comportment or behavior of a particular being called the "human." In its everyday signification, machination refers to a surreptitious or even enraged form of activity that busies itself with a calculated view to confusion or destruction. Such "machination" is at most a distant consequence of machination thought in terms of the history of beyng.

To know machination in its pure essence, not only insight into the historical essence of the κοινόν as the expansion and securing of empowering, but machination even over beyond the κοινόν.

Machination—power—overpowering.

*Its installation with a view to the unconditional subjection of all power to machination.*

The subjection of power, such that overpowering prevails in its essence as unconditional devastation.

### 42. Machination and Devastation[b]

The devastation that erupts from machination becomes most powerful when it even encroaches upon that which prepares its transition into something other, and which it has already abandoned in a concealed manner. Then each word that would endeavor to be said from out of a coming turns into a flood of public discourse that ensconces what is foreign with regard to such coming within the "new" of what is past, indeed as its "newest." Yet this encroachment on the part of devastation is really only an illusion. For in truth, the newest most emphati-

---

b. Ms.: *Devastation* [*Verwüstung*] = institution of the wasteland [*Wüste*], that is, of the instituted undermining of every possibility of any decision and of all realms of decision. The wasteland already is when everything presents itself as in order. Devastation as engendering the wasteland [*Ver-wüstung*] here does not merely mean the laying waste [*Wüstmachen*] of something present at hand.

## 42. Machination and Devastation [48–49]

cally belong in the middle of the wasteland, they simply take what is apparently other as an occasion to present their same old thing, and to sink altogether into decisionlessness.

The devastation itself remains immune to everything that disowns it and that has seen through its corrupted essence; for it cannot, indeed, be eliminated directly, but only set into its essential end through its very essence.

Machination empowers power into its essence. This essence, however, is overpowering. In overpowering there lies a suppression and annihilation. Annihilation here does not mean elimination or merely doing away with something on the basis of whatever is present at hand and holds validity; yet nor does it refer to a destruction or demolition in the sense of smashing into pieces what is at hand in the manner of a fragmentation. To annihilate here carries the "positive" sense of conducting into the nihilative. Because, however, the empowering of power as the unconditional must itself be such in kind, overpowering too is a complete annihilation. Completeness here does not have the character of summation, but of essence; it does not first take hold merely of all beings, but before that, of being itself. Complete annihilation is *devastation* [*Verwüstung*] in the sense of an instituting of the wasteland [*Wüste*]. Accordingly, devastation in no way refers to a merely consequential laying "waste" and empty of what is at hand, but rather to configuring the secured undermining of every possibility of any decision and of all domains of decision.

In this wasteland nothing "grows" anymore; beings no longer enter into the decision of being. Devastation does not create an empty "nothing," but is its ownmost kind of ordering: an instituted coercion into what is decisionless. Devastation is not lawless confusion or blind disintegration but has the assuredness that belongs to the self-instituting of power and indeed of unconditional power. The ordering force of devastation is wrath.

Devastation is in itself, not in its mere effects, wrathful. It empowers its wrath by aiming at a boundless duration of itself. The steadfastness belonging to devastation never coincides with the empty and impotent persistence of something lying at hand that has been destroyed; its steadfastness is not a consequence of a laying to ruin that has occurred and is thus "real." In its essence, rather, it prevails as the assured and impending threat of ever new impossibilities of a decision. Devastation is that which can never again be reversed, because it only precedes, and does so with a view to the extinguishing of every possibility of bringing beings as such before being.

The unconditional empowering of power in the exceeding of power gives rise, as this devastation, to the supreme power of the gigantic.

The latter too does not consist in a hitherto unattained excess of everything great and small. The gigantic has its essence in the instituting of a secured enabling of the measure-less, which can no longer make itself recognizable because it has undermined every attempt at delimitation. The gigantic that has been brought to dominance in the essence of devastation (that is, always of machination) becomes an unleashing of clamorous exaggeration and of secluded zealotry. The two belong together. Exaggeration, devoid of memory, proclaims each succeeding occurrence in turn to be the greatest and thoughtlessly proclaims every new measure as a unique accomplishment. Each time each and every thing is what is most decisive. And this all within the realm of an already long since decided, yet only now unfolding, decisionlessness. Zealotry flutters around as a sonorous bunch of uncomprehended statements and words from Hölderlin's poetizing and Nietzsche's thinking, words never interrogated because not open to being interrogated. A frothing brew of supposed incantations presents itself, mostly in hymnal form, as insight and knowledge, and claims to offer a guide accompanying "life." And everywhere these are merely forms of the devastation being instituted, forms with no power over themselves, and that further solidify their stubbornness through exaggeration being undertaken with a view to salvation and zealotry with good intent.

### 43. "Total" War

Once it has become public and ascertainable, one even finds that it is not at all "total," less so, indeed, than any war hitherto. Many human beings run around unharmed, for example. Only from time to time or on occasion does the war affect this or that person. In general, many a realm of everydayness remains entirely untouched after all. The war is being played out somewhere—in a space whose spatiality remains admittedly strange and hard to grasp.

The arguments brought forward here *against* totality in fact speak for it, and in such a way that we must ponder how inessential it remains whether the totality can be apprehended everywhere, directly and immediately, within beings; for totality is a title—although a bad one—for the *being* of beings, and in itself prefigures a configuration of beings that escapes our habitual experiences and for this reason is not ascertainable, so that the illusion arises that the total aspect of war indeed shows holes and is therefore not total.

# VI. The Sustainment[1]
## The Essence of Power
## The Necessary

---

1. Cf. *Κοινόν. Out of the History of Beyng.*

## 44. "The Dis-tinction"

of beyng in relation to beings is never "antithesis," such that a field for simplistic reversals could present itself here, for instance, of the following style: instead of asking concerning beings as such (metaphysics), we ask concerning beyng.

For *beyng* is not the Other in relation to beings, but *is* beings themselves, and *is* them alone!

Antithesis is possible, and even there only seemingly possible, only where being is taken as *beingness* and thought in terms of universalizations in relation to beings, and the universal and the particular, the individuated, are set in opposition to one another. Accordingly, one can distinguish ontic and ontological by way of introduction, but that *remains within metaphysics*.

## 45. The Trace Pointing to the Truth of Beyng[2]

Priority of beings without restraint.

And which being [*Sein*]? Machination; but unrecognizable within the realm of such priority.

Precisely such being is forgotten because singularly falsified into beings. *Power* as something that is a "being," and yet an unusual one. The unusual as the *first disruption* of the oblivion of being. In and through this, in opening up, the abandonment of being. In such abandonment the trace of refusal.

The latter as hint of being appropriated—the decision.

The essential prevailing of beyng, and truth.

The occasion of the unusual: the strange.

The strange and the usual. (The habitual and habituation.)

The usual: whether merely habitual and thereby forgotten, or whether especially in reflection; here already (steadfast insistent decision).

The usual—strange—as that which is *not active* and yet . . .

(From the strange, seemingly merely contemporary, into essential decision.) The usual unusual and the unheard of (in relation to the public and its noise).

---

2. Cf. Κοινόν. *Out of the History of Beyng.*

### 46. The Trace Pointing to the Truth of Beyng
### The Un-usual in the Essential Sense

is that which, within what is most usual, remains that which is overlooked the most and in advance—the being of beings. This, which is what is essentially unusual, does not lie outside of the habitual, does not fall outside of it, and is not some kind of fallout. For this reason too it can never be made familiar through such things. The unusual is the ground of the essence of the habitual, a ground that is concealed as such. When even the habitual is caught up in the frenzy of its corrupted essence and even this too has been forgotten, then there is no direct path leading to the unusual.

This name, admittedly, is a supplemental one and already something added on to our estimation—seemingly our exclusive estimation—of everything habitual.

First make our vision vigilant and clear for what is thus unusual. Our reflection is averse to all exaggeration and to everything that is sought. Letting the most simple and widely discussed relationships arise in inceptual purity.

In that which is strange, the unusual announces itself. What is more unusual to the human being who, in modernity, is banished into beings and oblivious to being, than *beyng?*

The readiness for granting a site to beyng.

### 47. The Truth of Beyng

to be grounded not for beings and so that the diversity of the merely diverse comes to dominate anew, but for the essencing of beyng itself.

The grounding of coming in carrying the abyss.

Beyng not to be derived, not to be explained. Every such intent is already mistaken in essence. Yet not mere "intuitus," intuiting, either; rather, *steadfast insistence of the grounding of truth.*

### 48. Beyng

is neither to be found before us in terms of "immanence," nor to be intimated through "transcendence." Neither path leads to the goal. Not at all because they are insufficient *ways,* but because they never posit beyng as the "goal" at all, but only ever seek "that which is" (a being as providing the standard, *subjectum,* or a being as that which is in the supreme sense: "God," or beings as a whole) in its beingness.

Beyng, however, "is" neither over us, nor within us, nor somewhere around us; rather, *we* are "in" it as the event. The intervening of beyng's arrival there in between.

And we *are* authentically (appropriated to the event of appropriation) "in" beyng only as those who steadfastly insist in *Da*-sein.

Being as the "wherein" is not "our," human "being," but the appropriative event of the in-between as the origin of time-space.

All appeal to existence, all "transcending" to "transcendence" (!) and all "acquaintance" with what is present at hand are through and through a relation to beings without knowing of beyng and without inquiring into the truth of beyng.

A relapsing into "Christendom," which has in the meantime gone through a process of secularization, as a schema for interpreting beings as a whole.

The "relapse" is fateful, not because it is a falling "back" and therefore not a moving "forward" in the manner of progress, but because metaphysics of whatever kind is not equal to the moment of the history of being, of being's abandonment of beings—indeed, not only not equal to it, but in thrall to it as handmaiden.

## 49. The Decision
### Beyng and the Human Being

Only one singular being relates directly to beyng—and this seldom.

Then, however, beyng entrusts its truth to that grounding that seeks in questioning.

The human being, who is that being in the manner of humankind, is then freely placed, in an inceptual manner, into a relation that is drawn into φύσις, or its humankind passes over into the other commencement of a transformation into that *Da-sein* whose essence must first be brought about in this manner (cf. *Contributions*).[3]

Humankind here means: letting beyng be unknown or the decision questioned in relation to its truth. This includes the destiny of belonging to a promotion of being's abandonment of all beings.

The supreme decision establishes itself where, in an inceptual manner, beyng relinquishes its ownmost truth to a grounding, and thereby at the same time casts off into the uncertain the possibility of a definitive dominance of the power of beings.

We are approaching this decision.

---

3. *Contributions to Philosophy (Of the Event)*. Gesamtausgabe vol. 65.

\*

In its initial projection (*Being and Time*), "Da-sein" is taken to be what is from here on "given" and then interrogated for such a projection.

And yet Da-sein *is* only in coming to be appropriated, and that is to say: essentially prevailing in that essential history that is just commencing.

Anticipatory thinking cannot fail to recognize such being appropriated, and must nevertheless attempt to acquire an initial concept of Da-sein, and to do so starting from being (along the guiding thread of the question of being) and from the human being, insofar as Da-sein can be assumed only by a particular humankind.

In truth, Da-sein is never "given," not even in a projection—unless such a projection prevails in its essence as one *thrown* in the throw of coming to be appropriated.

## 50. Decision

What decision is—
  Whence it springs forth—
  Whereby it is prepared.
  Decision and the trace of the event. (Being's abandonment.)
  The distinction between being and beings decisive. Yet in what way is this decision?
  The resonance of being in the unusual. But in what way the distinguishing?
  That *distinguishing* which by such a name seems only to be what is most vacuous, most indifferent, and most fleeting.
  How else the experience of its essence than by way of a steadfast insistence within Da-sein.
  The decision not between things that lie already pregiven, present at hand, but *between* that which first has to be brought to thought, brought thoughtfully to experience, its grounding brought about as the free site of a history. That is the priority of beyng and the grounding of its truth before beings.
  Never to be decided between a being or beings (which one also calls "being," for example, in the frequent saying "To be or not to be—that is the question"), that is, whether the human being is a being or not.
  But the issue concerns neither the human being, nor a particular being, nor beings at all, but rather whether beyng prevails in its essence.

*This de-cision the intimation of a pure coming*, today still entirely foreign and inaccessible and everywhere subject to misinterpretation, in case it ever should come into the first word.[4]
The vacillating while and the decision.
*Passing over into the era of the vacillating while.*
*Vacillating—hesitating—as the approach of coming.*
Hesitation and the unusual.
Hesitation and refusal.

\*

The decision belongs entirely in the essential prevailing of beyng itself. Yet beyng must in each case be grounded in its truth upon a humankind that leaves truth groundless, or itself for the first time knowingly assumes the grounding and does so in an inceptual manner, transforming itself into Da-*sein*.

The more knowing this assuming, the more purely it must initially be tuned, and that is to say, remain appropriated, by beyng.

Wherever this Da-sein-like, that is, instantiating, "decision" prepares itself, there it opens up the between for deed and knowing.

To be decided is: whether *"heroes"* still overpower beings and succumb to them, or whether *"wisdom"* enjoins itself to beyng.

## 51. Decision and the Future

Is the future only the ensuing and prolonged running its course of what is already present at hand yet hitherto scarcely experienced publicly, or is it the coming of that which not only absolves beings in the sense of those that are present and passing but that, as beyng itself, transforms the essence of beings and has already decided concerning all that is now and was then?

The decision no longer touches the outward appearance and formation of what is to come as the addition of new to old within the same world domain; it is grounding the essence of future itself.

Not whether we *are* and belong to those beings that make it through and are saved, but whether ever again, and more inceptually than ever, beyng may prevail in its essence.

The decision does not fall concerning something in the future, but first arises and is concerned with the *essence* of the future—and to-

---

4. Cf. foundational words.

gether with this, the essence of time. And the latter is just the preliminary name for beyng.

Not whether we pose or make the decision—that is impossible. But rather whether the human being can still be ready to prepare its arrival—or whether he must let it pass him by.

You may wander through all beings, nowhere does the trace of the god show itself.

For you only ever search where nearness already rushes by—the nearness full of the distances of the sustainment.

You can rearrange all beings, never will you encounter a free place for housing the god. You may even go beyond your beings and will find only the beingness once more of that which already counted as beings for you. You only explain, and all explaining falls back into an appeal to that which is in the first instance without question, that which, however, in its ground encloses within it all that is worthy of question.

## 52. Beyng

can never be told or described as a story. If its essence, first to be grounded, is its coming, then what corresponds to it is that questioning that inquires into the domain of the decision to be posed, opening up this domain, and coming to insist steadfastly within that which in its essence prevails as coming.

Technicity and historiography, unified in their essence and having arisen from the διανοεῖσθαι of the ὄν, still prevent a fathoming grounding that instantiates beyng, and will perhaps do so for a long time yet.

Yet we know the decision and its signs. Few as yet are able to distinguish what belongs to that which is to come and what lies suspended in the past, which as the present tends to confuse the two.

The event of being appropriated into the abyssal ground, since neither possession, nor robbery, nor any states of affairs pertaining to beings impose themselves where distance is released for the sustainment, and beyng the clearing of this distance itself and what essentially prevails in the carrying out of sustainment.

The event of being appropriated is essentially a coming; and not in the sense of being as *not yet* knowable by the metaphysical era.

Coming binds more essentially than every kind of presencing that merely appends itself and rushes over every interval and shatters nearness. For this reason, it is an error of metaphysics that consigns the essence of the senses to being "affected."

In beyng there is no hold or security, and therefore there is a coming to be appropriated into a reserve that cannot be exhausted in its bestowal.

"Interior" and "exterior" (of the human being) are just as little the "locale" of beyng, which in turn appropriates the human being to itself in a singular manner, without ever belonging to him.

## 53. *Beyng*

Machination and devastation.
    Devastation as the persistence of annihilation.
    The most extreme annihilation as being's abandonment of beings.
    The abandonment of beings as refusal of beyng.
    Refusal the most distant, inceptual bestowal.
    Bestowal as inceptual transformation of beyng.
    The inceptual trace of the essence of truth.
    Beyng is not itself "the Highest," is not itself the god.
    But beyng is the abyssal ground of its as yet ungrounded site, is the clearing sustainment (event)—de-cision.
    The time-play-space for grounding this site, the ground—appropriated—as Da-sein.

## 54. *Machination and Event*

From out of the first commencement of the history of beyng thinkers must *think ahead* into the most concealed moment of this history.

This moment determines itself through the decision, reserved for beyng, between the grounding of the truth of beyng and devastation as the instituting, through machination, of a definitive abandonment of beings by being.

Such thinking alone "*thinks*," steadfastly and questioningly insists within the essence of truth, insofar as this essence is itself decided in the decision.

Such thinking ahead is the sole historical thinking, one that thoughtfully anticipates the *essence* of history. Whatever else today is called thinking is either "historiographical" explanation, or dissection, or "biological" calculation; everywhere decisionless.

## 55. *The Singular Decision*

is that between the *decisionlessness* set in power through machination and the *readiness for decision*.

The decision concerns that which is de-cisive. That is beyng, whether beyng turns toward de-cision.

The decision cannot be "made." One cannot "wait" for it, rather, the site of its essencing is presumably to be engendered through grounding.

The de-cision is, and that is to say, as the appropriative event comes to appropriate Da-sein or withdraws beyng from every truth.

### 56. Whence Being as Power?

From out of being, which became objectivity ever since "actuality," ἐν-έργεια, and even before that since the ἰδέα via the *actus* became *perceptum* and represented-ness.

Behind objectivity there concealed itself for a long time, up to German Idealism, more precisely, to *Schelling*, being as will—and the "will" as the spiritual-psychological code name for power.

How both are prepared in Leibniz: *perceptum* of *percipere* and *percipere* as *appetitus*, all in the full essence of *vis activa primitiva*.

That being became power and had to become such is authorized by its own essence, which since the first commencement had to forego the grounding of its truth and thereby the essence of truth. Why this foregoing? The consequence of departing from the excessive fullness of the first inceptual commencement. Power wreaks power. Being as power is the corrupted essence of the first inceptual, ungrounded essence of being as φύσις.

### 57. The Essence of Power[5, a]

1. Power's overpowering each attained level of power and thereby bringing about the essential prevailing of its ever-veiled essence: that is
2. the empowering of itself in overpowering, the exclusion of every outside that is not itself. Alone determining the essence of beings.
3. For this reason, power is without "goals," without anything that, as *not* it itself, could ever determine it; and on the same grounds neither "goal-less" in the sense of an errant wandering around among "goals" that fundamentally are, after all, sought, nor "arbitrary," for everything that serves power is its right and its will, all already chosen and proposed for it. In this manner, it can never at all be evaluated, so long as it is comprehended as power.

---

5. Cf. *Κοινόν. Out of the History of Beyng; Mindfulness.* Gesamtausgabe vol. 66, §9. Machination, §65. Beyng and Power; foundational words.

a. Ms.: Cf. now also: *On Ernst Jünger, "The Worker"* (67ff.). Gesamtausgabe vol. 90. Edited by Peter Trawny. Frankfurt am Main: Vittorio Klostermann, 2004.

## 57. The Essence of Power [63–64]

4. Power needs no bearers, because being is never borne by beings, but rather at most the converse: beings are empowered to themselves in a thorough-going manner by being, that is, by power. Above all, it has not yet been recognized *that*, and still less comprehended *why* power, in order to prevail in its essence as being, needs no bearer.

   Wherever we still see power in the hand of the bearers of power, it is not yet power itself that is borne there, but only ever a "means" for the empowering of power, a "means" that is compelled and determinately attuned by power. Power needs no bearers and can never have such in general because it is never a being that could be ascertained or represented here or there. It is being itself, in each case unveiled in a different way, and in which all beings (the kind that are effective), whether transparent or not, oscillate. Being as power unleashes beings into mere effectiveness (force, violence, and the like), and precisely in such unleashing, power is unconditional power. Being can never be "borne" by beings in such a way that being would rest upon beings and be by virtue of their mercy. Power, rather, prevails in its essence within itself as being and is squandered by beings into becoming effective and is unceasingly confirmed. Power cannot be seized (taken possession of), because we can only be possessed by it, since it is *unconditional subjectivity*. (Cf. regarding Ernst Jünger.[6])

5. All those who have power only ever "have" means of power, institutional arrangements of beings corresponding to power, arrangements that are themselves beings. They never "have" power because they are "had" by it.[b]

6. Power annuls the possibility of "right," insofar as "right" is comprehended as a claim on the part of that which is relevant in itself and therefore valid, and in this way removed from power.[c] Yet the institution of power will least of all tolerate a right-lessness. Annuling the possibility of "right" here means the adaptation of its essence to a title for the distribution of power.

7. Power is something other than the manifestation of a "force" and is more essential than every kind of might. Its essence is nonetheless still regarded in terms of force and capability, and thus essentially underestimated, even when it is understood as "spirit." Power is a prevailing of beyng's essence and can therefore never

---

6. Cf. *On Ernst Jünger, "The Worker."* Gesamtausgabe vol. 90.
b. Trs.: Having—as possessing, disposing.
c. Trs.: To what extent is power removed from right?

be explained in terms of bearers; in the age of metaphysics it can only be experienced, but never authentically known.
8. As overpowering, power is always building ahead—("constructive"). Where the "constructive" becomes lodged in the mastery of beings, what becomes manifest is that there is no longer any escape in the face of power as being in beings. Beings must submit themselves to power, together with the builders, who are only able to play with scaffolding, without ever being grounders. What remains essentially withdrawn from them is felt obscurely as a lack that, in the domain of power, can never at all be admitted. To the contrary, the erection of scaffolding as being thrust by power from one makeshift to another presents itself publicly and to itself as a building for "eternity."
9. Power and force.
10. It belongs to the essence of power that its essence *is* an impelling into truthlessness, that truth in its essence (as clearing of beyng and question-worthiness of being) is destroyed.
    What is least conspicuous, least pondered, and a matter of supreme indifference is what is decisive in the powering of power. The truthlessness of beings under the unconditional domination of power is not a *consequence* of power, but the self-unfolding non-ground of the essence of power itself.
11. Overpowering is the non-resistance belonging to power in the face of its being impelled into the unceasing exceeding of each attained level of power. In terms of power, non-resistance is of the nature of a *command;* command and the security of command as the veiling of the enslavement to truthlessness that lies within power's domination.[d]
12. Power attains the supreme level proper to its essence when it not only determines what "is right" (namely, whatever has actually been attained through its "success" as that which is valid), but when it also sets down what "greatness" and "struggle" means: "greatness": supreme domain of power, reckless in its effects; "struggle": suppression through the technicity of power, for the sake of power, in which process "goals" merely play the role of means for power and "methods" of "struggle."
13. Power admits as its other only impotence as its sole other, and in this decree, since it has everything within its power of "de-

---

d. Trs.: *Command*—as an unconditional correspondence in the face of the empowering of overpowering, pure subservience in the face of empowering. Command has the unconditioned, not on the basis of a grounded sovereignty but on the basis of a groundless, unconditional servitude toward the essence of power.

cision," is assured of the agreement of all, even of the impotent. The most severe limit of the essence of power lies in the fact that it cannot look out beyond itself, because it is not permitted to do so in accordance with its essence.

That power can demonstrate its supreme essence only on the grounds of being's abandonment of beings says how decisively the essence of power in its unconditional character depends on beyng and nothing (more nihilative than every nothing) would be without beyng.

14. The opinion that power could ever be eliminated in history, however, springs from the same oblivion of being as that consciousness on the part of power of being the sole and true ground of historical humankind and of having to be ever anew. Any other relationship to power is not possible within the era of metaphysics, and the event of an overcoming of the essence of power, given its indispensability in institutional terms, cannot even be intimated.

15. Toward a reflection on the essence of power
"Power" must at once be extricated from the framework of "political" considerations and positions and factions.
"Power" can only be interrogated metaphysically with regard to its essence; and even this only once the essence of metaphysics has already been recognized and its commencement (beginning), and in this way its consummation, experienced.
Power then unveils itself as the essential prevailing of machination, and the latter as the hidden essence of "efficiency" in the metaphysical sense, which is rooted in the interpretation of being as ἰδέα—ποίησις (φύσις—οὐσία). (Cf. On the History of the Concept of Existence.[7])

16. Power and Impotence
Impotence thirsts after power and degenerates from lack of power. It is bound into the essence of power in the manner of privation.
Impotence can, therefore, in turn become a power by availing itself of a reversal.
It can likewise give rise to the illusion that it is without need of power and an overcoming of power in its essence.
Impotence: the most insidious illusory essence of power.

17. On the essence of power
The sole, yet then at the same time also unconditional impotence that essentially belongs to power as the innermost cor-

---

7. In: *Vorträge*. Gesamtausgabe vol. 80.

ruption of its essence, is found in the fact that it is unable to have power over its own willfulness, which, in keeping with the needs of the oppressed in each case, and for their appeasement and the confirmation of their "importance," must continually furnish historical images that are not merely "false," for instance, but that above all obliterate any kind of reflection.

18. To what extent the full unfolding of the essence of power first begins with the unconditional character of its essence.
   To what extent this unconditional character necessarily includes the unconditional domination of mediocrity.

19. Power and Freedom
   The *metaphysical* essence of the unconditional empowering of power's essence shows itself in the fact that the unfolding of power lays claim to a fundamental principle for itself, one that metaphysics repeatedly proclaims: freedom is necessity. This thought allows one to address as something necessary all force and everything forcibly brought about and kept suppressed by power's violence, and to interpret such necessity as freedom. Thus, whoever is forcibly suppressed knows himself to be free, and in such self-consciousness will renounce any uprising against what is necessary, which is to say, against coercive forces. For how should one who is free want to rob himself of his very freedom.
   The manner in which the metaphysics of unconditional power, in its consummation, has recourse to this principle at the same time shows the intrinsic, essential connection between *power and illusion*.

20. Power and Illusion
   The power that exempts nothing from its assumption of power nonetheless prevails as power precisely with the aid of *illusion* also, as though *it,* power, first set "free" those who are overpowered, delivering them over to the vocation that they themselves hitherto remained incapable of attaining. Thus there arises in those who have been overpowered the "feeling" of themselves first attaining *their* own legitimacy. They fail to notice that in the meantime they have been transposed beforehand, through the process of overpowering, into an interpretation of their "selves" that is in accordance with such overpowering. This *illusion* of liberation is the most stubborn compulsion that the essence of power is capable of accomplishing for itself.

21. Power and Veiling
   Power can also proceed to exploit to the full precisely all that it denies and combats, and at the same time to mask this ex-

ploitation, since one cannot conceive that power would continue to support and nourish itself from the very thing that it has overcome. Here too power finds yet another way to bring its "creative force" into the spotlight through the hidden exploitation of what has been created previously, and to extol itself as the discoverer.

22. Power[8]

The innermost essencelessness of power, as the most extreme corruption of its essence into which being has unleashed itself as beingness, consists in the fact that it is unable, and not permitted, to have the power to admit any essential opposition to itself.

Power [*Macht*] is not only im-potence [*Ohn-macht*] but the corrupted essence of being in the form of the singular machination of beings. Cf. *Mindfulness*[9] and *Overcoming*.[10]

To what extent does power essentially maintain itself in indeterminacy and thus in the possibility of every disposing over every setting of goals?

Herein lies its ownmost determinacy and unequivocalness of essence that is alien to all who are impotent and yet in its counter-essence also proper to them.

23. Power

The essential restlessness of power as over-powering conditions the fact that power is "will" to power, namely in such a way that will as command subjects itself to this restlessness, so as to withstand it as such and to make it constant.

As a consequence of this restlessness of power, power can never ground sovereignty in the sense of the prevailing of laws from out of the "ancient joy" of the essencing of beyng itself. All power is illusory sovereignty; and for this reason it is also incapable of bearing any "opposite" that is in any way essentially inceptual.

(*Sovereignty* is the χάρις of beyng as beyng, quiet worthiness of the gentle binding that never needs to calcify into the need for power.)

"Sovereignty" thus becomes an entirely inappropriate word and for this reason assigned over to the essential domain of power.

---

8. Cf. §41. Machination (conceived in terms of the history of beyng).
9. *Mindfulness*. Gesamtausgabe vol. 66.
10. "The Overcoming of Metaphysics." In: *Metaphysics and Nihilism*. Gesamtausgabe vol. 67. Edited by Hans-Joachim Friedrich. Frankfurt am Main: Vittorio Klostermann, 1999.

24. Power[11]
The essence of power unfolds itself as machination into the unconditional.
The overcoming of power.
Machination is the essencing of being that is ungrounded in its truth.
And for this reason, the essencing of power is the extremity of metaphysics, and here the decision conceals itself as to whether being itself comes to be true as beyng of that which is essentially Other to all power.
To do battle *against* power means still to place oneself under power and its essence, and that necessarily demands in turn resourcefulness on the paths and means of power (μηχανή) in the primordial sense. Where power does not yet appear as such in the manner of modernity.
Power is in essence overcome only through that which is in no need of power. Only being itself, taking itself back into its essence, lets collapse those beings that have elevated themselves to domination within being's unrecognized abandonment.
Only when power runs into the nothing, when it can no longer even "make" an opposition for itself, does it collapse within itself and its essence.
When beings can no longer appeal to their being used and maintained and enhanced in order to "justify" being, which only drags being's essence down to a means.

25. Power and Race
The *thought* of race, that is to say, the reckoning with race, springs from the experience of being as subjectivity and is not a "political issue."
Racial breeding is a path of self-assertion for domination. This thought is accommodated by the interpretation of being as "life," that is, as "dynamics."
The cultivation of race is a measure in keeping with power. It can therefore be deployed at one moment and put on hold the next. The manner in which it is implemented and promulgated is dependent upon the state of domination and of power at any given time. It is by no means an "ideal" in itself, for in that case it would have to lead to a renunciation of power claims and promote the validity of every "biological" predisposition.

---

11. "The Overcoming of Metaphysics." In: *Metaphysics and Nihilism*. Gesamtausgabe vol. 67.

## 57. The Essence of Power [70–71]

Strictly viewed, for this reason within every doctrine of race the thought of the *priority* of a race is already entailed. The priority grounds itself in various ways, but always on something that the "race" has accomplished, an accomplishment subject to the standards of "culture" and the like. Yet what if culture, when assessed from the restrictive perspective of racial thinking, is only a product of race. (The circle of subjectivity.)

Here the self-oblivious circle of all subjectivity comes to the fore, which contains a metaphysical determination, not of the ego, but of the entire essence of the human in its relation to beings and to itself.

The metaphysical ground of racial thinking is not biologism, but the subjectivity of all being of beings, which is to be thought metaphysically (the scope of the overcoming of the essence of metaphysics and of the metaphysics of modernity in particular).

(Too crude thinking in all refutations of biologism: therefore futile.)

26. Power

In determining all being of beings, it denies humankind every possibility of coming to itself, which is to say, of still experiencing being a self at all as possible ground of truth.

Power tolerates no equalizations. It stakes everything on the either-or of subsisting or not subsisting, even where, namely due to more far-reaching reckoning, it seemingly lets something subsistent still rest in itself temporarily. Power pursues the most extreme either-or, and only for reasons of power does power hide the fact that its essence demands the "life and death" struggle and drives in this direction. The one must annihilate the other. Yet he thereby robs himself of the very possibility of experiencing a corresponding "recognition" through another humankind that would be commensurate with the height of his own power. Because this possibility falls away, even the victor can find no recognition; he himself sinks to the level of the mere presence at hand of one who merely has an effect. Every possibility of a truth is destroyed.

The essence of power as machination annihilates the possibility of the truth of beings. It is itself the end of metaphysics.[e]

---

e. Trs.: *Power and worldview;* worldview and consummation of metaphysics.

## 58. The Determination of the Essence of Power

The way and perspective in which the essence of power is determined here are not taken from the narrow perspective of a historiographical and political way of viewing things. What is determinative comes solely from beyng-historical thinking. That is to say: the manner of questioning does not proceed from "power" as a "manifestation" that can be encountered precisely here or there, so as then to delimit its essence. This thinking, rather, emerges from a history of inquiry into being, and in this history experiences that, and how, being becomes actuality, self-representing effecting (subjectity), knowing willing, and ultimately "will to power." The will to power must be thought as the consummation of the (metaphysical) truth about beings, and thus as being. Only then can it be recognized how, within the will to power, the essence of power is intended as being. Yet this very comprehension of power as being must, as beyng-historical, think ahead into the overcoming of metaphysics. Only from here can light be shed on the essence of power in such a way that this essence is removed from the restricted sphere of a domain of beings.

Thinking ahead into the consummation of the truth of beings from out of the overcoming of this truth recognizes the essence of machination. Machination, for its part, however, has its as yet concealed essencing in the fundamental trait of being in accordance with which beings are relinquished to being's abandonment and surrendered to the seemingly exclusive rank assigned to beings over all being.

The levels of the beyng-historical thinking that attempts to think power in its essence, and in whose own history the essence of power is inquired into, and can be inquired into only there, may be indicated by the following sequence:

Being as actuality.
Actuality as subjectity.
Subjectity as the will to power.
The will to power as being.
Being as power.
Power as machination.
Machination as the unleashing of beings to themselves.
The unleashing of beings and devastation.

Insofar as this thinking starts in a seemingly arbitrary manner with the determination of being as actuality, it may be recalled that the history of being can present itself in a history of the concept of "existence." Within this history, a knowledge may be attained of the extent to which actuality as *actualitas* points back to ἐνέργεια and thereby to the inceptual first commencement of the history of being. Yet why

## 58. The Determination of the Essence of Power [73–74]

did being have to disseminate itself into the essence of power? May we ask concerning a why here? Is that the correct orientation toward what is determinative?

\*

In order to be able to think the essence of power as being, therefore, the thinker must first have relinquished in advance the desire to come to know any particular "manifestation" and in the wake of such knowledge to lay out a stance that may be taken toward "power." The thinker must remain within thinking, that is, in renouncing explanations of beings by way of beings, he must keep to the relation of being to him, the determination that essentially prevails within beyng. Only then is the possibility granted of finding the essence in relation to the essence of power. Otherwise, in counting on explanations of power, we are stuck with and repeatedly arrive at only condemnations of power or glorifications of power or an indifferent coming to terms with it as something unavoidable.

This kind of argumentative thinking about power can never reach into the sphere of its essence and cannot even intimate the fact that in the essential prevailing of power a history of being itself and "only" this history is running its course.

The essential prevailing of power finds its consummation in power's becoming unconditional self-devastation through overpowering compelling itself, in the complete emptiness of unhindered powering, to undermine every possibility of a commencement within the realm of its essence. This supreme unfolding of the essence of power, however, by no means appears in the guise of the devastation and destruction that are otherwise familiar, but in the semblance of their opposite. Signs of the consummation of the essence of power that can be ascertained historiographically are "planetarism" and "idiotism." The "planetary" refers to the relation of power's essence to the entire earth, and indeed in such a way that this relation is not the result of an expansion but the beginning of a unique domination of the earth. The "idiotic" (ἴδιον) refers to the priority of that which is addicted to itself, which initially gives itself the stamp of subjectivity.

Because power has instituted within itself an essential hostility toward everything that belongs to commencement or that ever again turns back toward the commencement, power stands opposed to all dignity. Power and dignity are indeed named together from time to time, and where power is represented before one as the possession and adornment of a being, glory seems to belong to power as domination, and to glory, dignity (*majestas*). What is experienced everywhere here are undeveloped pre-stages of power within beings, beings which have being in the efficiency of making.

Thought in its essence, however, dignity remains so decisively alien to power that it may not even be posited as its opposite, a move that after all ascribes to both the sameness of a sphere of essence.

Dignity is the revealing of concealing, a revealing that holds itself purely toward the intimacy of the commencement, maintaining a remoteness out of this intimacy, returning into the commencement and turned toward this return.

The dignity of what belongs to the commencement is attained by no power and is never knowable on the basis of any power.

### 59. Power "Needs" Power (Violence)

The needing is ambiguous. Power requires power as a means, in order to be power. When power puts itself to use and has to use itself up, then power becomes violence. However, violence is not necessarily or always an act of violence, yet it is always a forcing. The violence that has not been unleashed in its forcing, and which does not degenerate into a blind thrusting and blocking, is nevertheless violence, and thus nothing other than a forcing into the unfree, a forcing that is needed by power and put to use, yet in a harnessed or veiled manner.

Power, however, requires power (the exertion of power that uses power) not only as a means but "needs" itself (is in need of itself) as the goal. For it is power itself that must bring itself to bear and "to power." And this overpowering of itself is the overflowing superfluousness of its own emptiness that is proper to it. In such a way, it is in itself superfluous beyond itself and at the same time in each case in need of itself as a means.

In the fact that power is essentially at once goal and end and means and mediation, it contests the essential stock of what belongs to institutional production and to malleability in general. In so doing it demonstrates its fundamental trait of constituting the essence of effectiveness as actuality.

Every exertion of power, in which a "violence" is not simply applied as an available "active substance," first transposes beings into the domain of power and determines beings in their aspect of power. This occurs even when beings are violently subjugated and "stripped of power."

Every power claim and every form of staking such a claim, precisely because their own kind of being arises in them and thus threatens an alienation and consternation and thereby a weakening of power itself, requires a pretext through which the essentially violent essence of power remains veiled. This covering over of the violent essence of power, which "moralistically" may readily be condemned as a "lie," cannot, however, be comprehended in moral terms at all. For it belongs to the essencing of being. Because one only ever regards power in terms of beings and as a being, and as the irrupting of one being into beings that are otherwise secure and habitual, however, all judgments concerning power take refuge in a condemnation of the exertion of power and in indignation concerning it.

That the unfolding of power and exertion of power on the grounds of the metaphysics of modernity provides modern humankind with "ideals" and erects as "ultimate goals" first "social justice," then the "progress of culture," then the saving of Western "culture," then a new "world order," then a political system—all of this is not a greater or lesser, more or less skillful hypocrisy stemming from some other obscure sources of human action; rather, this incommensurability between what one says and what one "really means" is demanded of every possessor of power by the essence of power's empowering. Those who have power must pay a due that surpasses every other "sacrifice," and they must pay it often, in that they are furthermore not even able to know the obligation to pay dues in which they stand.

## 60. Power and Violence

Violent activity (brutality) is distinctive by virtue of a peculiar simplicity. Its operation aims at unconditional annihilation by means that are unconditionally effective on every occasion and in every respect.

Thus, as soon as two powers with equal capacity for brutality clash with one another, it will be apparent that their methods do not differ in any respect, because there is nothing there with respect to which they can distinguish themselves at all. For this reason, the possibility also intensifies here of responding at a stroke to the opponent's operation using corresponding means.

Through all of this, that is, through the capacity for brutality unleashed to an unconditional degree, future clashes themselves become quite "simple"; they attain unconditional callousness, which then has only one path of escape remaining, the path that leads back to unconditional callousness itself. Annihilation becomes an end in itself.

## 61. Power and Crime

Where power becomes historical as the essence of being, all morality and legality are banished, and indeed unconditionally. Power is neither moral nor immoral, it unfolds its power outside of morality, law, and custom. Everything that is cultivated, preserved, and maintained in these domains, everything that is demanded here and set as a standard is unconditionally shattered by power itself, and shattered in such a way that nothing else takes the place of what has been shattered, other than power itself—which, however, as being, presents itself as the ungraspable nothing, which is why the shattering of everything permanent and enduring must display this extreme of destruction.

For this reason, the great criminals belong to the era determined by the unconditional essence of power. They are not to be judged by moral or legal standards. One can do so, but then one never arrives at their real criminality. Nor is there any punishment that would be great enough to discipline such criminals. Every punishment essentially fails to measure up to the essence of their criminality. Even hell and the like are too insignificant in essence compared to what the unconditional criminals bring to ruin.

The major planetary criminals, in accordance with their essence and as a consequence of their unconditional servitude toward the unconditional empowering of power, are entirely alike. Historiographically conditioned distinctions that circulate widely as a foreground serve only to cloak their criminality in the harmless and even to portray its accomplishment as "morally" necessary in the "interests" of humanity.[12]

The major planetary criminals of the most recent period of modernity, in which they first become possible and necessary, may indeed be counted on the fingers of one hand.

---

12. At this point the following statement appears in the manuscript: "Zu fragen wäre, worin die eigentümliche Vorbestimmung der Judenschaft für das planetarische Verbrechertum begründet liegt." This controversial statement was omitted from the first and second editions of the German text but is scheduled to be included in a forthcoming third edition. The meaning of this statement is a matter of dispute, but it translates to something like: "One would have to ask what are the grounds that peculiarly predetermine the Jewish community for planetary criminality."—Trans.

## 62. The Essence of Power and Subjugation

In power, "spirit" arrives at its most extreme and unconditional unfolding into the unrestrained corruption of its essence. "Spirit" here means in the modern sense: the self-knowing knowledge that is the actuality of everything that acts.

For this reason, only ordinary understanding can remain stuck in the superficial aspect of the merely "negative" and fail to recognize being itself in the essence of power.

Thus it happens that one attributes "power" to certain "bearers" and makes them responsible for what they "do" "with" power, instead of pondering the fact that the bearers are the servants who are made solely by power.

Yet in keeping with the essential unfolding of the essence of power into the unconditional corruption of its essence, the "servants" are no dwarfs, but rather *"giants,"* namely with regard to the manner in which they *subjugate* themselves absolutely—without comparable measure—to the essence of power. What is giant concerns the open resolve to subjugation under the essence of power and the inability to know the essence and origin of the necessity for such resolutions.

## 63. "The Demonic Nature of Power"

One tends to be especially fond of speaking of this when one thinks one possesses a "vital" notion of "actual" power. In truth, however, this idle talk is the best testament to lack of insight. Talk of the "demonic nature of power" presupposes that power is "really" and "naturally" justifiable and necessary within certain limits, but would just have to be "morally" constrained and guided. One at first thinks of the essence of power in terms of a shallow equating of power with "violence" as permeated by morality and, then, from the lack of moral control, lets its "demonic nature" arise.

The cluelessness of this notion of power is characteristic of the usual schoolmaster judgments of historians concerning history.

## 64. Power and Truth

As being, power must empower an openness, and here that means the public, and thus bring to power the essence of "truth" appropriate to it. As a consequence of the modern configuration of the essence of power, true means as much as correct, and correct means the empowering of power that secures as secure and guaranteed. Whatever does "justice" to this empowering, commanded and controlled by it itself, is true and is so in each case only to this extent and to this degree. True means as much as doing justice to power's empowering.

Yet because power is in each case unconditional, so too its truth in each case is never conditional or relative. For this truth, there is nothing further in addition that could grant or demand other criteria of judgment. Because anything else is banished in advance, the truth that belongs to power is "unconditional." For this reason, power in the public communication of its truths must also always "adhere to the principle of unconditional truth."

What power ascertains is on each occasion unconditionally correct in relation to whatever fact is focused on and selected for communication. There is no other regard for other things in terms of which or within which what is said would at once have to be only conditionally correct. All statements of power are unconditionally true. For this reason, wherever diverse power positions stand opposed to one another, each one independently states its unconditional truth. None of them lie. And yet all of them lie. Thought more precisely: since on each occasion each one is unconditionally true in the said sense, this kind of power-truth must also on each occasion be unconditionally false. Still more clearly: whether true or false in the sense that something is in each case determined in *each* respect, this "whether-or" is inessential for power. The "true" can also quietly be, and even must be, the false, for the false too is not that upon which power grounds itself or in terms of which power could let itself be assessed and judged. The true is really only that which is in accord with power. To speak here of a use readily leads one astray; for it is not a matter, either, of something useful for someone or some purpose. The point is the empowering of power, and the true is true not as something useful but as something powerful in itself.

One can be filled with moral indignation concerning this kind of truth, yet one must know that this is not a response that is commensurate with power. Nor can a retreat to the moral ever fathom the ground of this essence of truth, which was recognized, moreover, by Nietzsche, in its beyng-historical essence, or prepare an overcoming. With the aid of morality, one can only evade, and that means, exclude oneself from history, which proceeds via the unleashing of the essence of power into machination.

The wretchedness of Christendom is most clearly manifest in the fact that it swings back and forth between unconditional power positions and offers its services to one or the other depending on need in each case.

Here it also becomes recognizable that within the realm of vanishing Christendom a decision about the godhood of the gods can never take place. It cannot even be intimated.

### 65. Power and Leveling

"Power" seduces us into the view that its essence is realized in supremacy and domination, and thereby also in subjugation and even suppression. Accordingly, power brings inequality with it. This is also the case, so long as we look only at the beings that are determined by power. If, however, we think the essence of power itself, that is, if we understand it as being, then it at once becomes manifest that to power there belongs an essential equalizing, and this in an unconditional sense. Every power empowers in the same direction, namely, into the increase of power, which as a process of overpowering concerns its own essence, and does not mean the subjugation of beings. The increase of power, however, already for the sake of its own security, requires the greatest possible uniformity of "principle," so that this uniformity of the essence of power entails the homogeneity of power and the enforcing of an equality in the entire expansiveness of power. Thus it comes about that wherever power struggles unfold ever more purely, where purity means ruthlessness in the unleashing of power's essence, the opposing parties bring themselves reciprocally into the complete equality of themselves.

### 66. Power and Wretchedness

The customary view links the possession of power with the unfolding of splendor and showmanship. This hits on something essential with respect to the manner in which power must maintain itself in the public realm, for through splendor it creates viewers and participants in the festivity, who in this way (powerfully through power) are brought into the view that they themselves are partners in power and its co-bearers; the role that the "people" is permitted to play in the publicness of power's splendor and of the possession of power.

Within the history of the unfolding of the unconditional essence of power, "socialism" is therefore necessary, but with equal necessity it can never be "a mere 'socialism'" by itself, but rather is always a ... socialism. What is attached to it as a prefix as the real ground of power can assume different variations, and, seen in terms of power, is not absolutely decisive either. The point is simply a form of social order that grants unconditional rule. This permeating of the people by power, who are publically declared to be the sole bearers of the will, is a preemptive and unconditional disempowering. It belongs to it that it act precisely without splendor, without the many forms of ostentation, without becoming entangled in mere institutions on account of the greatest possible wretchedness. To the possession of power and its display there belong splendor and din; to the essence of power and its own securing there belongs the greatest wretchedness. This wretchedness requires an extensive superficiality of thought. It is best served by thoughtlessness. This wretchedness gets by without "culture." For this reason, in the decisions concerning power, and that means the planetary possession of power, it is not the depth and greatness of "culture" and "education" and historiography and the like that gets decided, but a resolve in favor of the wretchedness of the most basic rules of the game in accordance with which the means of power are ruthlessly brought into play.

To the wretchedness in the unfolding of power's essence there corresponds the leveling belonging to power. In its wretchedness power has the ground for the tenacity of its essence.

All this brings to the fore the unconditional emptiness that lurks within the essence of power itself as the most extreme unleashing of being into the corrupted essence of beingness.

This emptiness is not nothing, but rather the ruthlessness of power even toward itself, since the point is always an overpowering. This ruthlessness and emptiness then gives rise within the public realm to the impression that really anyone can do what the possessors of power accomplish, that there is nothing to it, other than—supreme servitude within the accomplishment of power's essence. And this is rare; a rarity corresponding to the fact that power too is foundational essence, the corrupted foundational essence of being, and the latter, by way of singularity, remains within its own.

### 67. *"Power" and "System"*

The first thing that strikes common understanding is that power works and operates according to a "system."

In this view, which power itself imparts to our everyday opining about it, there lies, however, a fundamental deception. In its essence, power is systemless, and precisely this secures for it the powerfulness at all times to remain certain of its overpowering of itself. By contrast, that to which power, in itself systemless, lays claim for itself is the possibility of total organization, which never assumes a commitment with regard to beings, and indeed denies beings in advance any claim to a commitment. What is routine for the essence of power, not being bound to beings and the way in which they are assessed and evaluated on each occasion, is repeatedly felt by everyday opining to be something strange, which it seeks to debase as a "lack of principle."

## 68. Power and Public

Power needs the public, but with the intent of confusing it through and through, and of undermining the possibility of forming an opinion. The result of this confusion is complete indifference toward everything. The greatest successes no longer cut any ice, and at most stimulate vacuous curiosity to look toward the next, which have already in advance been credited with being inessential.

Such indifference *seems* to endanger power and its capacity to act. In truth, however, power becomes only more powerful, for unconditional indifference makes it possible for everything to be permitted. In this way, within the essence of power itself and through this essence, the counter-essence to power indeed arises, as the only thing against which power shatters: unconditional lack of resistance. It brings it about that power suddenly powers into its own emptiness and overpowers itself into the nothing.

## 69. The Inhabitual and the Unexpected

In periods of unrestricted planning, which is satisfied only by ruthless measures, the calculability of all beings is attributed to them as the fundamental characteristic of their malleability. Yet this attribution is by no means a "subjectivizing" of the "objective," because the subjectivity of the human being's comprehending and asserting himself as *subjectum* indeed already corresponds to the essencing of being in the sense of malleability, namely, in such a way that only thereby does something objective, beings as objects that *stand* over against the setting-before of representation, first come to be grounded upon a ground that is inaccessible to the metaphysics that proceeds in this manner.

Where calculability has become the sign of beings, the unexpected is the rule. For all the planning processes in service to calculation penetrate into a wasteland that they themselves do not control, but only ever exploit and use up; uncontrollable by themselves, these processes must collide with one another and thus give rise to that which can never be planned. Yet the unexpected is in each case only the corrupted essence of the inhabitual in the guise of the surprising exception and of the deviation.

### 70. The Necessary

1. The unavoidable—uncircumventable—inalterable—that which must be taken on; that to which one then either *succumbs* as it crushes the human being or to which one succumbs by standing in resistance to it—without regard for oneself and without prospect of change. Standing in resistance does not mean a withstanding, but a standing up to that which crushes.
What is essential here, therefore, is how one takes oneself. In *recognizing* something as "necessary" in this sense, one attains a position only insofar as one is placed in a position to decide or not to decide for oneself.
Here is the place for the naked *heroism* that merely affirms the unavoidable, but is incapable of anything more. This can mean a great deal compared to the pitifulness of attempts to avoid or anaesthetize, and compared to the harmlessness of falsifying and the shortsighted "pessimisms" and "optimisms."
The necessary in the sense outlined admits of no possibilities any more, a process in which the possible is circumscribed and calculated within the perspective of what has gone before, of those beings that are dominant (and their being).
Yet the necessary in this sense does not decide and precisely cannot decide whether it itself is perhaps merely the last possibility of what has gone before, and thereby not at all something necessary that is coming, but rather, that merely accomplishes its passing by and passing away. For essentially other is
2. the necessary in the sense of that coming whose ground is unfathomable, which conveys within itself the purest openness of the most simple decisions, not unavoidably, but rather binding to a readiness for the coming.
For what is necessary in the first sense referred to, need is only the lack of escape; and this kind of the necessary does not turn this need, but forces and compels into it.
For what is necessary in the other sense referred to, the need is that there is no appropriative event of the openness of the undecided yet decisive transition; and this kind of the necessary thrusts into the

clearing of need-lessness and turns, that is, transforms the need in the manner of a setting free into the free site of essential decision.

## 71. Beyng-Historical Thinking

is appropriated from out of beyng itself, which prevails essentially in pure coming. Yet this does not make its action into a passive suffering or mere intuiting. The opening of appropriation lays claim to the supreme accomplishment: the leap, a questioning one, into the clearing of the abyss. What is sought after in questioning is the essence of truth. And insofar as the event of the decision concerning this essence is inceptual history, thinking remains historical from the ground up, and must therefore let itself be carried from the first commencement, via the end of the consummation of metaphysics, out into the other commencement, by the ungraspable carrying force of those words whose bearers we do not at all need to know. Such thinking must think two hundred years ahead in order for the first Germans to awaken into a site cleared for the decision between the truth of beyng and the precedence of beings that has become a wasteland. And for a long time the direct trace will be lacking that points the paths within the simple neighborhood of the rare moments of the history of beyng.

We are to ponder neither that which is past (only beings), nor that which is eternal (only beings) as a refuge and escape—thinking must enquire after beyng alone, as that which is undecided yet replete with decision.

Thinking—as enquiring after the truth of beyng—must, in its saying, press ahead into the realm of the coming, inceptual decision, as the sole place where it encounters the trace of the event.

Thinking must, therefore, pass through being's abandonment. Yet before this, such abandonment must first be experienced; and for this what is first required is, in turn, the shattering of the oblivion of being. The occasion for shattering through the clearing of the inhabitual. The latter conveyed in what is strange.

The strange as disruption of the habitual.
The habitual and the usual.
*Habituation.*
*The inhabitual* in the sense of *beings* that are surprising and odd.
*The inhabitual* in the sense of beyng that long since prevails in its essence and requires no intermediary.

Beyng-historical thinking neither brings solutions to enigmas nor does it create reassurances in matters of need. It is the steadfast insistence within the essence of truth. What more essential may otherwise be demanded of thinking?

Beyng-historical thinking is always *inceptual* thinking; it never loses itself in any kind of historiographical report on the course of opinions or doctrines.

In every leap the trace of inceptual history is sprung open, a history that carries into its kind, and that means: into the commencement, the other one, which, as the commencement of beyng, is now the *sustainment* itself, the essencing of the truth of beyng.

Beyng-historical thinking plies itself to that which is form-less, it is granted no reliance on "image" or on the thing that elucidates—stark and bold is its word.

For the task is to ground an intimative generation within what is owned by beyng.

Attuned from the start by beyng, the thoughtful word must keep silent its voice.

Inceptual thinking not only initiates the commencement, it also remains within the commencement and only ever points into it. The *soundness* of this pointing is everything; the didactic unfurling of catchy ideas, its greatest danger.

*Beyng-historical thinking* is a thinking along multiple traces; neither mere representation, nor its multi-level guise in the sense of the "dialectic." The "dialectic" can easily serve as a means for misinterpreting the thinking along multiple traces, and yet it is even more removed from it than inceptual νοεῖν is from φύσις.

Thinking enquires after the manifold traces of beyng, which, as event of appropriation, unfolds its essence in a simple, onefold manner into the mani-fold of the sustainment.

Every trace of beyng points toward others that follow, but they are never, ever, to be thought at the same time, that is, this is never re-presenting or intuiting, but rather in each case instantiated readiness for a path toward the abyss.

## 72. *The Essence of Philosophy*

and the respective history of a thinking, in the sense of the grounding of history it has taken on, can never be explained in terms of the "personality" of the "philosopher"; still less is such "personality," as distinguished from what the thinker has thought, that which properly remains. Only historiographical biologism, extended into the metaphysical (the "subjectivity" of the human being) can spread such erroneous views. It should not surprise us that Nietzsche fell victim to this "tendency" and first made it "modern."

Presumably, by contrast, the comportment of a thinker can indirectly provide the pointer toward a stance that for its part indicates the way in which the relation to beings is in general determined and attuned. And what is unveiled therein is the manner in which beings essentially prevail as such—which truth the truth of beyng is of, and whether it is grounded or not.

Thus a hint concerning *Heraclitus* may be able to say something essential concerning inceptual thinking, that is, the history of beyng; granted that one "reads" and understands him neither "biographically" nor "historiographically" at all, but experiences him *historically:*

ἀναχωρήσας δὲ εἰς τὸ ἱερὸν τῆς Ἀρτέμιδος μετὰ τῶν παίδων ἠστραγάλιζεν. περιστάντων δ' αὐτὸν τῶν Ἐφεσίων, 'τί, ὦ κάκιστοι, θαυμάζετε;' εἶπεν. 'ἦ οὐ κρεῖττον τοῦτο ποιεῖν ἢ μεθ' ὑμῶν πολιτεύεσθαι;' καὶ τέλος μισανθρωπήσας καὶ ἐκπατήσας ἐν τοῖς ὄρεσι διῃτᾶτο [. . .].[13]

## 73. *The Human Being and Da-sein*

The human being: the animal that has reason.

Reason: *either* borne and driven by animality and for the furthering and inhibiting of "life" *or* guiding and steering the animal aspect yet still incorporated into the latter. "Values," "goals" conceded, but human; "contents" that in one way or another fill out the formal and properly functioning aspect "of life."

---

13. Cf. Hermann Diels: *Die Fragmente der Vorsokratiker.* Edited by Walther Kranz. Volume One. 5th edition. Berlin: Weidmannsche Buchhandlung, 1934, 22 A 1, 140 (Diog. IX 3). Translation in the lecture course of summer semester 1943. Cf.: *Heraklit. 1. Der Anfang des abendländischen Denkens. 2. Logik. Heraklits Lehre vom Logos.* Edited by Manfred S. Frings. 3rd edition. Gesamtausgabe vol. 55. Frankfurt am Main: Vittorio Klostermann, 1994, 10: "He, however, had retired into the sanctum of Artemis, to play the knuckle game with the children there; here there now stood the Ephesians round about him, and he said to them: 'What, you scoundrels, are you staring at in such astonishment? Or is it not better to be doing this than to concern oneself with the πόλις together with you?'" What follows is translated by the editor: "And finally he spurned human beings, left the common way and lived in the mountains [. . .]." Translated as *Heraclitus: The Inception of Occidental Thinking. Logic. Heraclitus' Teaching of the Logos* by Marnie Hanlon. New York: Continuum, 2013. Translation modified.

The life-functions are what is constant, the remainder a result and a filling out on each occasion.

Everywhere the human being—worldless and unearthly—, without his belonging to beings as such ever grounding his essence, indeed in such a way that "life"—body and soul—are co-conditions of the accomplishment and course, the prolonging and curtailment of his essence.

That belonging to beings, however, must now first be elevated to the level of what is decisive, to the extent that the truth of being becomes worthy of question and a grounding of this truth as Da-*sein* is to occur.

Then an essential transformation of the human.

Possible only after the most extreme and extensive shatterings.

VII. The Essence of History
"Commencement"
"Beyng"

*74. History*

is the coming of that which comes, and for this reason alone also the past of that which goes and the having been of what has been, and thereby also the presence of whatever is passing. History is this, not in piecing together the three different "temporal" aspects but rather from out of the essential ground of such coming. The coming springs from the event as the essencing of beyng.

History is the history of beyng, and therefore history of the *truth* of beyng, and therefore history of the *grounding* of truth, and therefore history as Da-sein; and because Da-*sein* is instantiated only through the guardianship of a given humankind, the human being is historical. His historicality essentially unfolds in his belonging to the truth of beyng.

Such coming is to be projected in its essence in terms of the refusal that is dawning amid the devastation.

*75. History*

as "happening," not with a view to processes and movement, but rather the suddenness—sheer and precipitous—of grounding from out of the event.

From where does this come? From the *singularity* and simplicity and seldomness of the event (cf. Hölderlin's intimation in "Voice of the People").

The gigantic aspect of events and the improbable character of history.

Today the word "happening" is used for anything and everything, and "*history*" as a word must therefore be restored to its essence.

*76. History*

as history of beyng (i.e., as grounding of the event) not only knows no going "back," it knows no "*forwards*" either; for there is no such thing as either the former or the latter. In this history and as it there prevail the *sudden moments of founding and precipitous collapse,* and the "between" is the duration of occurrences as veilings of the preparations and unwindings: the corrupted essence of suddenness.

Suddenness, however, does not mean the same as the temporal νῦν of the fleeting now.

Suddenness has its own *expanse,* and at the same time its corrupted essence in the un-suddenness of the immeasurable that remains veiled from itself—*devastation,* for instance.

*

The history of beyng, as the first inceptual history of metaphysics, must pass through the devastation.

Global destruction and the shattering of order are mere foreground to devastation. If they remain absent or are deflected, devastation is merely all the *more* prevalent, that is, deceptive.

### 77. *The Essence of History*

In *Being and Time*[1] the attempt is made to project the historicality of *Da-sein* on the grounds of temporality.

Da-*sein* is historical only because it is essentially and properly the grounding of the truth of beyng as event.

The event is the prevailing essence of history, and from its relation to sustainment in the sense of steadfast insistence, Da-sein is essentially historical.

In *Being and Time* this connection is presupposed, intimated, but not mastered, nor is that the initial task. Temporality [*Zeitlichkeit*] temporalizes the realm of the clearing for being (Temporality [*Temporalität*], as it is called there[a]). Temporality [*Zeitlichkeit*] is the preliminary name for the truth of beyng, which as event is the essencing of "history." For this reason, "temporality" must come to be the ground of the possibility of the "*historicality*" of Da-sein.

So long as history is conceived proceeding only from Da-sein, it has indeed been grasped essentially and in a manner incomparably different from every perspective of historiography and its "object." Despite this, the essence of history does not yet come into the free here and in this manner; and for this reason no grounding decisions can yet be made from this perspective regarding the historicality of Dasein.

*History is grounding of the truth of beyng, and in such a way that this grounding as such is a coming to be appropriated in the event as sustainment.*

Da-sein is steadfast insistence within history, and for this reason the humankind that steadfastly insists within Da-sein can be authen-

---

1. Cf. *Mindfulness.* Gesamtausgabe vol. 66, §79. *Being and Time.*
a. Trs.: The epochal I. 3.

tically or inauthentically historical, where inauthentically historical means "unhistorical."

Yet insofar as it is shown that humankind has not yet at all been appropriated into Da-sein, and indeed because being's abandonment reigns within beings, it must be recognized that this humankind is as yet *without history*, and for this very reason is "historiographical" through and through.[2]

Because Da-sein first prevails in a futural-transitional manner, all that was and is *before* this commencement must be historical in the sense of the as yet concealed and ungrounded relation to the truth of beyng. And insofar as this relation must have been forgotten before this, the transition traverses a "time" without history.

*The age of the world without history, and devastation.*

Plant and animal are *not even* without history, because they do not stand in relation to history in any way whatsoever.

## 78. History (Past and Having-been)

Bodily and biological descendence from earlier generations gives no right to the claim to be the possessor and preserver of their history.

The living are rejected and denied by the living. Here, an essentially other grounding is needed, one of pro-venance [*Her-kunft*] (as historical) by way of the future as the to-come [*Zu-kunft*].

Everything here is either mere progress, radical change—or the suddenness of the commencement. The commencement alone gives rise to a withstanding the essence of beyng as *the abyss of history*.

History is only where a decision takes place, each time inceptual, concerning the essence of truth.

## 79. The History of Beyng

In the essential prevailing of its truth, beyng gifts the *essence* of history which, of such an essence, is *its* history.

History cannot be regarded here as a kind of maneuvering with beyng, a maneuvering that gives rise to events; history is inceptually the possession of beyng. Beyng attunes and determines a relation that is incomparable in kind. History is opened up in its essence by beyng, and in this opening up of its essence, beyng brings itself to its truth.

---

2. Regarding historiography, cf. *Mindfulness*. Gesamtausgabe vol. 66, §64. Historiography and Technicity; §62. History.

Yet beyng is never "the Absolute" or "the most universal," neither the highest nor the lowest—nor can it be computed in any of these habitual, that is, metaphysical perspectives.

The utterly incomparable, unattainable through any relation and therefore set loose in its essence, in this sense *Ab-solutum,* ab-solute, yet never the highest nor the slightest, but rather solely and singularly of *its* own essence.

## 80. History and Beyng

The opening grounding of essential pliancy in beings, which ad-mits something coming in its singularity.

Beyng is the appropriating of the essence of history.

History is not something made by humans, not at all related to humans originally, but assigning itself to the *Da-sein* through which the overcoming of the human is afforded.

The most coming of that which comes is the *coming of the last god,* to whom history conducts beings as a whole for a most far-reaching ad-mittance of its decisions.

## 81. Concerning the Essence of History[3]

History not from the perspective of *historiography,* as its object.

History not as one domain of beings, distinguished from *nature.*

From where, then, is it to be determined from which essential ground history is to be determined?

If we posit "history" as that which is worthy of question (in its essence), into what prevailing opinion do we then place what is referred to in this word? We surely mean something in an indeterminate way, and do not cling to an empty word. And why is "history" worthy of question?

Whence the claim of this prevailing opinion and its truth?

To what extent is *temporality* essential for the essence of history? (cf. *Being and Time*)

Not because "happening" runs its course "within" "time," but because "time" has an essential relation to the truth of beyng[b] and his-

---

3. Cf. "The Overcoming of Metaphysics." In: *Metaphysics and Nihilism.* Gesamtausgabe vol. 67.

b. Trs.: The epochal I. 3.

tory is the essential prevailing of this truth; *time as the time-space of the clearing.*
Can this be proven, and what would a proof serve here?
Which truth is proper to the grounding of essence?

## 82. Commencement—History—
## The Suddenness of the Commencement

Every commencing is different, in keeping with the essence of commencement. What does commencement mean? *To be the abyssal ground of history.* Abyssal ground—that which releases what can be grounded into its essence, in such a way that that which releases refuses itself in the process, denying to the grounding anything present at hand or an appeal to or ossifying in such, but rather imparts to it as its own the necessity of decision. In deciding, insofar as it is a matter of essential decisions concerning the essence of being, there is a going back into the abyssal ground. Such decisions themselves transpose themselves into something unprotected and without support.

If the essence of beyng as event is addressed *to* reflection, then beyng brings itself to word, without being able to be stated in the manner of explanation.

History is essential prevailing of the truth of beyng. Beyng itself, and only beyng, is in turn the abyssal ground of this essential prevailing.

"Commencement" encloses within itself the richest mystery of beyng. Only a commencement can recall a commencement and bring it into the word.

## 83. Essence of History

That beings that have been kept out of the truth of beyng and unsettled may be grounded in their essence and come to be set free in the grounding of Da-sein.

That a moment of such possibility may *pass by* uncomprehended, *this non*-occurrence is essentially historical compared to all those things that can be listed that transpire and are "experienced" in the form that "one" *says* and *proclaims* that one has a lived experience of such things.

*Passing by,* however, is here to be known from out of the essence of beyng, which as refusal does not permit itself the slightest influence in machination. Here, passing by does not refer to a process that transpires in such a way as to be objectively ascertainable. Passing by is said from out of the knowing of being's abandonment of beings that reigns within machination.

## 84. "Life" and "History"

Life has no need of the concept in order to bear its vitality, but "life" remains excluded from the relation to beyng. Such being excluded lets it belong to its own essence in its *own* way.

Relation to beyng: what does that mean? (*Being*-human). "Life" is surely also a manner of being—yet without that relation.

Each and every being comports itself *differently* toward its essence; from this it also becomes clear already that determining the essence as κοινόν never attains the truth of essence.

If the ground of the human essence is the relation to being, then the transformation of the human being can come only from the transformation of this relation. The relation transforms itself, however, from out of that to which it relates—namely beyng and the fact that beyng essentially demands its truth as something to be grounded.

## 85. Historiography

is the settling of accounts with the past in relation to the present, in such a way that the present remains futureless, admits nothing that could come *toward* it—affecting its essence—in a transformative manner. What is admitted as "future"[4] is that which has been calculated in advance, already made secure and consequently the exaggerated "eternity" that goes with it.

The settling of accounts with the past consists in representationally referring whatever is worth knowing about it to the measures and representations of the present. This settling of accounts stands in the service of that calculating that institutionally directs whatever is present. Settling accounts with the past thus becomes the training of one's contemporaries to do whatever satisfies their "interests." These "interests" themselves extend only so far as the present that is slipping away distances itself from the being of beings and rolls itself up into a growing self-securing and its refinement.

The settling of accounts with the past, historiography, that is, is the *technicity* pertaining to that which cannot be pursued in a machine-

---

4. Cf. §51. Decision and the Future.

like way. This *technicity* is for its part pursued through "politics." All historiography is "political," not in the superficial sense that it predominantly has "political" events as its *object* but through the fact that—whether consciously or cluelessly—it maintains itself within the service and mechanism of the total planning of "life" trained to secure itself. Even "literary history" is, in a technical-political sense, incapable of ever venturing a relation to history. It is "political" even where it appears indifferently to examine and explain "works" "in themselves" and avoids any crude idea of a purpose (the feeble aim of "folklore" and the like).

## 86. History

How history as the essential prevailing[c] of the truth of beyng is appropriated singularly in the *event*.

How the latter itself is to be enquired into thoughtfully in singular trajectories.

How all setting into relief of that which is familiar and of beings must be renounced.

*History is* the truth *of beyng.*

History is eventful appropriation of the *clearing.*

*Clearing*—rapturous sustainment of the struggle of countering and strife.

*Sustainment and singularity.*

*To be—the clearing—*casting oneself into it as open = *Da*-sein.

Da-sein *is* history—"is" *historically.*

Historically, that which lets the essence of history essentially prevail.

## 87. History[5]

as eventful appropriation, the essential appropriative events, the recollective clearing of history.

Never in terms of what is past, never in terms of historiography and its objectifying representation of the past for the present; the referral of the latter to what is past.

---

c. Ms.: What is meant by "essential prevailing" [*Wesung*]?

5. Cf. *Überlegungen* XII, XIII. In: *Überlegungen XII–XV (Schwarze Hefte 1939–41).* Gesamtausgabe vol. 96. Edited by Peter Trawny. Frankfurt am Main: Vittorio Klostermann, 2014.

Eventful appropriation and recollection.
Recollection and having been.
(Seemingly, and thought in an everyday manner, what has been is most decidedly of all "away" and bygone—that which is most past.)
Whereas in the beyng-historical concept of essential having-been [*Ge-wesenheit*], the essence [*Wesen*] first carries back to itself.[d]

## 88. *The Essence of History*

as essencing of the truth of beyng.

Starting from here, the *historical* essence of "thinking" is to be conceived from the ground up, and a preparation ventured for a steadfast insistence within this history.

Overcoming metaphysics wholly as such history.

*

History alone is historical. As essencing of the truth of being, it gives rise to the essence of truth in different stages of grounding. Such opening up of the essence, the closer it comes to beings and runs its course within beings, becomes a possible object for historiography. In its essence, historiography has nothing in common with history; the latter can never be comprehended in terms of the former.

---

d. Trs.: Prevailing of essential having-been [*Ge-wesung*].

# VIII. Beyng and the Last God

## 89. The Last God

That which is most coming in coming, the appropriating that sustains itself as event.

Coming—as the essence of beyng.

Coming and suddenness.

Coming not empty or errant but as refusal, clearing of its own accord the time-space *of poverty*.

Coming and the event.[1]

Ask beyng! And in its stillness, as the commencement of the word, the god answers.

You may wander through all beings, yet nowhere does the trace of the god show itself.

## 90. The Countering

The gods and the human being extend their essence from opposite directions into beyng, and in this way alone can counter-ing essentially prevail in the event of appropriation.

The gods need beyng—in which sense?

The human being belongs to beyng—in which manner?

The gods "are" not, and yet need beyng as the abyssal ground of being cast back upon themselves.

No single being is capable of accomplishing such a thing.

Being cast back, however—whence its necessity?

## 91. Confidence and Dasein

Being mis-taken in one's essence with a view to what is most coming.

The essence of joy, this confidence attuning the fundamental attunement of serene magnanimity and intimate forbearance.

This confidence strong enough to take up into its essence *being terrified, seized with horror*.

Being seized with horror, and devastation.

---

1. Cf. *Überlegungen* XIII, §81, §89. In: *Überlegungen XII–XV (Schwarze Hefte 1939–41)*. Gesamtausgabe vol. 96.

## 92. Beyng Is . . .

Beyng is—      event of appropriation
                  ↓ ↓ ↓
               sustainment
beyng's ability    de-cision              un-binding
to be sustained                           assignment
                                          into the sustainment—
                                          the latter as

                   abyssal ground
coming and the     nothing
refusal[a]         poverty                poverty and dignity—
(for in each case [?]                     power-less sovereignty
*not*-coming!)                            inceptual
                                          *dis-appropriation* of
                                          beings and
                                          their supremacy
                                          *out of coming to be*
                                          *appropriated*
                                          into the abyss.
                                          The power-less![2]

attunement         stillness
opening of
appropriation and
attunement

                   truth
toward the open    "in between"
and public         time-play-space
sustained—         clearing "of" sustainment

Beyng—*sustainment*—clearing (the concealedness of refusal) the abyssal ground

Singularity of beyng[3]

---

   a. Ms.: Refusal (cf. [. . .]*). Keeping to itself of the sustainment. What is this? The coming of what is most of all coming. *[one word indecipherable]
   2. Cf. *Mindfulness*. Gesamtausgabe vol. 66, §65. Beyng and Power. Still a historiographical and metaphysical perspective!
   3. Cf. *Mindfulness*. Gesamtausgabe vol. 66, §49. Beyng.

## 93. Event[4]

brings the untraveled expanses of world that must first be grounded into the draw of the open in tearing us away,
places the earth back into the steadfast peacefulness of pure closure,
raises both into the strife that concordantly liberates each, as most remote, into its own,
in sustainment clears the abyssal ground whose unextracted configuration is traversed by impoverishment into poverty,
essentially opens that Da-sein in which the arrival for the coming of what is most coming is grounded and the countering in relation to the last god springs forth.
Carrying out of sustainment—*being appropriated.*
Event: the essence of beyng raises this (beyng) into the most remote precursiveness.
Event of appropriation—and stillness—word.

## 94. Earth and World

The distinction is a beyng-historical one. It does not set off one present at hand thing against another, but rather thinks a history of beyng out of which earth and world ground themselves *historically.*

Every earth closes itself off and thus belongs to a world; closing itself off is its *earth-like* character, but earth is, furthermore, historical and already historical. An error to think that one could say something about "nature" or comprehend it independently of history; the impossibility of such in-itself comprehending does not signify any "subjectivism."

Every world opens itself and remains configured to an earth. Every world and every earth is thus historical in the entirety of what belongs to it. This history, however, in keeping with the history of beyng, is seldom and simple and, as that of the Western world, already configured from out of the essence of beyng.

The history of the earth of the future is reserved within the essence of the Russian world, an essence that has not yet been set free for itself. The history of the world is a task assigned to the Germans for *reflection.*

---

4. Cf. *Mindfulness.* Gesamtausgabe vol. 66, §16. Beyng, 83; *Überlegungen* XIII, §6ff. In: *Überlegungen XII–XV (Schwarze Hefte 1939–41).* Gesamtausgabe vol. 96.

History itself is here in each instance the unitary history of beyng, and indeed the essential prevailing of its truth, in which earth and world find themselves in entering the strife that is their origin.

## 95. Beyng

is event of appropriation, propriates itself.

"*How*" the event of appropriation "is"—as though it were a being—is a question that cannot be posed. For beyng *is—authentically,* that is, out of being appropriated and as such being appropriated.

"*When*" the event of appropriation is and "where" it is always remains an inappropriate question, for "time" and "space" in the original sense (of the clearing of time-play-space in the sustaining counterplay), and especially in the greatly derivative sense, spring forth from the event of appropriation, *are* together with it.

So beyng, then, is "supra-temporal" and "supra-spatial"—no! Rather, as abyssal ground it is the most temporal and spatial—*the time-space dimension of clearing* as site, indeed as sustained in sustainment, *the abyssal ground of the in-between:* abyssally temporalizing-spacing as appropriative event.

If we ask "when" and "where" and "how," we imagine something that "is" and fail to speak from out of the history of beyng, to watch over the truth of the event of appropriation, to ready a preparation for grounding the "decision" concerning our belonging to the history of overcoming.

## 96. Beyng

is *de-cision* in the sense of delivering into sustainment.

The de-cision is not "made," but rather opens in arising as event of appropriation.

## 97. Beyng and the Nothing

appropriates eventfully the time-play-space of that history that prevails essentially into the nothing that has sprung forth from it itself and essentially prevails only together with it.

Gods and humans who oppose the essential prevailing of the nothing rob themselves of their own essence and remain only figures of beings, to whom the truth of themselves, the truth of beyng, remains denied, and all that is left over is to wear themselves out in the busy production of machination.

So long as steadfast insistence within the nothing goes essentially unrecognized and is not acknowledged as being directed into beyng, and so long as the nothing is not yet said as a name for that in the direction of which the magnanimity and forbearance of reflection, ready for decision, exceed one another, then all hoping and longing assumes a defensive posture toward the coming of what is most coming. The veiled battle that rages in the consummation of modernity between "vital interests" and "eternal bliss" as they seek supremacy or even balance is only the most underhanded means through which machination solidifies its domination.

## 98. Beyng
### Coming to Be Appropriated into the In-between

The in-between (as in the midst and meanwhile: having the character of time-space) is that wherein countering and strife themselves essentially prevail between one another, that is, cross one another.

This *in-between* (the There of clearing) is the essential prevailing of beyng itself—that which has been eventfully appropriated to it.

This essence of truth first grounds something true in each instance.

Coming to be appropriated into the in-between brings beyng into its essential prevailing and casts what is oppositional into its dissonance.

## 99. Poverty[5]

Dis-appropriation from beings and the supremacy of their power, a disappropriation that is not robbery or removal but rather the essential consequence of an eventful appropriation of beyng in its truth. The intimacy of this eventful appropriation is the bestowal of the essence of beyng into sustainment, a bestowal removed from all need and deprivation.

Poverty is the inexhaustibility of bestowal, abyssally decided from out of itself.

Impoverishment *out of poverty,* the grounding of Da-sein that springs forth in such impoverishment, is history.

*Poverty: the essence of beyng as eventful appropriation.*

*The owned—as the essence of "beings."*

---

5. Cf. Beyng and power, the power-less. In: *Mindfulness*. Gesamtausgabe vol. 66, §65. Beyng and Power.

Impoverishment—enclosed in the eventful appropriation "of" Da-sein as steadfast insistence and watching over truth is a belonging to history as the history of beyng.

## *100. Poverty*

not being in need, not lack of means. In that case it would be merely a breaking off and taking away, merely a relation of deprivation to something other that is refused, whereas it is indeed not a relation and not deprivation, not a directedness toward what has been withdrawn, yet nor a mere reversal, a *wealth,* but rather the eventful appropriation of the proper essence of beyng.

*Poverty and the owned.*

Because we know nothing of it, we avoid its supposed threat and do not venture the safekeeping of the gift of impoverishment.

# IX. Essence of History

## 101. The Beyng-Historical Concept

The beyng-historical concept is a *comprehensive concept* [*Inbegriff*]:

1. not the collective representation of a universal, stated in an inventory of delimiting features;
2. yet also not simply the inclusion of the one comprehending (the human being) within what is conceptually comprehended, with the result that the human being is someone affected by the concept (still by what it refers to), rather
3. a comprehensive concept in such a way that beyng is thought as eventful appropriation of the sustainment, and thus on every occasion demands fundamental decisions and each time a different steadfast insistence within them.

Thinking in comprehensive concepts says beyng in every leap. It necessarily retrieves itself into singularity and its wealth.

## 102. Beyng

Beyng first conveys, at the same times of its concealed history, the middle of the essence of the human being and appropriates this middle over to the relation to beyng, a relation that is not representation, nor any mode whatsoever of lived experience, but rather the grounding, at times yet to happen, of the truth of beyng. This middle of the essence of the human being is nowhere and never independently present at hand but rather first comes to be in the event of the human being's being appropriated into Da-sein. The human being cannot "make" this history and can never intervene in it; seized by its essence, the human being can only prepare the time when what is most coming in the coming will strike him from out of the remoteness of the nearest. So long as the human being remains outside of this preparation, he totters back and forth at the end of a long dead end; he has forgotten to strike out on the path back—back, that is, not into the past but into the commencement, whose antecedent reign Western humankind has directly evaded.

## 103. The History of Beyng

History is the history "of" beyng, appropriated in its essence by the latter. This being appropriated, however, is the essential essencing of beyng itself—the event of appropriation.

*History is temporal opening up of the space of sustainment.*

"Time" and "space" are here to be thought in terms of being as commencement, from *rapturous removal and clearing* and from the essence of truth, accommodating spacing as granting the jointures of de-cisions.

History as the history of beyng does not mean a sequence of occurrences to which beyng falls prey (not that which "happens" to beyng), but rather that which beyng as such essentially opens for itself, insofar as it is the abyssal ground of "truth"—of its essence and corrupted essence.

Only the history opened up in its essence by beyng, and indeed already in the manner of a first commencement, then becomes the history of beyng in the sense that it casts itself forth into moments of temporalization, singular and rare moments.

The essential prevailing of history opened up in its essence by beyng is the grounding of the truth of beyng.

That into which beyng (essentially) bestows itself is impoverishment into that poverty entrusted with its simplest wealth.

\*

The history of beyng to the beyng of history.

The commencement as refusal.

The other commencement: bestowal into impoverishment unto poverty.

History first *is* as grounding of the truth of beyng, a grounding first appropriated by beyng.

If, however, history is, and whenever history first is, then the appropriation of beyng occurs as appropriative event. *Da*-sein, and it alone, *happens*, prevails in its essence as appropriated in the event, in temporalizing ground and site and guardianship for the event of appropriation.

(The essence of history cannot be deduced from a "happening," from occurrent events or the accomplishment of actions, but is determined in terms of the event of appropriation as the *essence* of history, that is, as that which is in the first instance openly appropriated.

Beyng and its essencing decides regarding the essence of history.)

\*

The history of beyng, as soon as this history brings itself into its essential grounding, is the axial site in whose field the priority of beings and the power of correctness shatter in favor of the mildness of beyng from out of the essential unfolding of the clearing of sustainment.

The thinking that is opened and attuned by beyng (beyng-historical thinking) is never the mere inversion of the metaphysical thinking that has been undertaken hitherto but rather the relinquishing of metaphysics altogether through the turning of questioning into the essential unfolding of history as that axial site.

Thinking is "of" beyng, and thus attuned opens, in its saying, the truth of beyng as sustainment into the simplicity of the word that keeps silent.

History: impoverishment into poverty.

The grounding of Da-sein that springs forth and accomplishes itself from out of such impoverishment. (Cf. poverty as essence of beyng.[1])

## 104. History of Beyng

only in the derivative sense to be regarded as the thinking of beyng, insofar as thinking is here taken as the human accomplishment of a still current representing (yet even then never as a historiography of opinions concerning the beingness of beings).

History itself conceals itself in its essence through various stages. These differ in each case in accordance with their origins, as do the grounding and abyssal grounding of the truth of beyng.

History determines being human only for the reason that and to the extent that, insofar as and because the human being is enjoined into his essence by his relation to beyng, which is essentially and singularly historical.

History:
as essencing of truth,
as Da-sein,
Da-sein and *"godship,"*
not human, not divine,
yet "more" than the human and "less" than the god.

\*

Beyng as being appropriated (appropriative sustainment) into the abyssal ground.

---

1. Cf. §100. Poverty.

Therein lies the essential decay of everything ground-like in the sense of original cause and of *explanation* and derivation, not even *causa sui*.

\*

On the path of questioning there lies not only that which is questionable, undecided, but: the decision for the "to come" [*Zu-kunft*] of beyng.

### 105. Bestowal and Reflection

The event of appropriation, as which beyng, as refusal, bestows itself.

This bestowal, as *history,* happens only where there is an inceptual thrownness of Da-sein, though precisely not grasped as such—*rather?*

(*Being attuned over* into a simple necessity.)

*Being freed for the awaiting* of the bestowal of beyng. In what way?

The leap into becoming reflection on the truth of beyng.

Inceptually-abyssally concealed: beyng.

Historically: the indirect and singular overcoming of machination, and thus in advance a *disempowering* of every intent belonging to machination.

Without claim, without measure, and yet enjoined into something decided, emanating the inexhaustible character of its simplicity.

The inceptual coming to be appropriated into the disappropriation of the truth of beyng (φύσις, metaphysics).

### 106. The Joint Crumbling of the German and Russian Worlds through Machination

Russia—that we not assail it technologically and culturally and ultimately annihilate it,[a] but set it free for *its* essence and open up for it the expanse of its ability to suffer the essentialness of an essential saving of the earth.

---

a. Trs.: i.e., not physically wipe out, nor even defeat militarily, but deprive it of its own concealed essence through renewed and radical implication in the machination to which we ourselves have fallen prey.

## 106. Joint Crumbling of the German and Russian Worlds [119–120]

That *we* prepare the impoverishment into poverty as the wealth of beyng and are strong enough to bestow it as a gift.

In this way alone do we surrender ourselves to the essential unfolding of a strife that compels the human being into its future.

Precondition: Being freed for ourselves, overcoming of modernity.

More essential than the critical encounter of the Greeks with their East, for now there are *two things* in play at once for us:

reflection on sense [*Be-sinnung*] as the leap into supreme thinking and

as being attuned to the simplest thrownness of Da-sein.

These two things are something singular—which the *future holds in store*.

Deception too must grow to the scale of the gigantic, as though the singular future of Western history would *also* succumb to the adjusting and installing of machination. Indeed it must and it will.

Only this proves nothing against this future, but is only a sign that something other is first required.

A great, precipitous, *historiographical assault* upon *Russia*, a limitless, ongoing exploitation of *raw materials* for the intricacies of the "machine."

The danger is not "Bolshevism," but rather *we ourselves* in that we impose upon it its metaphysical essence (without comprehending it as such) intensified to the extreme—and *deprive* the Russian and German worlds *of their history*.

Purely historiographical and political accounting in two directions at the same time: hope and fears—however!

# X. The Owned[1]

---

[1]. Cf. §100. Poverty.

## 107. Bestowal and Impoverishment

Being as appropriative event appropriates Da-sein into its essence (first founds it against the nothing). In this opening of appropriation, the event bestows itself as a gift in the manner of refusal (it never emerges to the fore as something representable in a possible objectification). Such bestowal is im-poverishment (an essential letting become poor) in the wealth of the singular, as the manner in which beyng prevails in essence by contrast with all beings. Im-poverishment into essential poverty bestows the ground of possible steadfast insistence within Da-sein, to whom alone care belongs, yet care is the truth of beyng.

Such care is abyssally different from every gloomy or wretched worry. It is the essencing of wealth in the simplicity of its bestowal into the owned in which beings of beyng (as event) find their essence.

That to supreme bestowal there corresponds impoverishment—to know this is a fundamental demand of beyng-historical thinking.

## 108. The Owned (Beings in Beyng as Event)

belonging to the opening of appropriation, distributing the simple *wealth* (unfathomably simple in the manner of abyssal ground) of the contentious and of counterance.

Beings in the sense of the owned are never what is *actual* in the sense of what can be straightforwardly encountered in setting it forth and setting it before us.

The contentious and counterance are never to be grasped dialectically, because they are never to be apportioned representationally, in the manner of properties, to mere oppositional statements.

"Nature" and "world" in their metaphysical stamp are incapable of saying that which pertains to the owned, of experiencing strife as the site of grounding the time-space of countering.

Strife as site of the nearness of an awaiting what is most remote.

Even "thing," "tool," "work" are still metaphysical—and fail to bring what they name into the in-between of beyng. Whether not here something simpler, singular, in accordance with stillness.

Strife as site of countering, gift of counterance.

Countering as freeing what is contentious.

## 109. The Owned

Only what is owned that comes out of singularity is something essential. Yet where singularity in turn springs forth from the opening of appropriation, there belongs to it the simplicity of that which is abyssal in ground and never to be exceeded.

It is from out of the singularity of beyng that we must first experience the alienating character of beings as owned.

## 110. The Owned

*Earth, world, human, god.*
  In what terms are they differentiated and distinguished?
  Upon what ground? which is experienced *how?*
  As abyssal ground of the event of appropriation.
  Must not these designations *also* collapse as metaphysical?

*Whence the distinction of the human?* From the assignment of his essence into the *most extreme possibility,* which, nowhere groundable within the sphere of a being, speaks wholly from out of beyng to the human in his unrevealed essence: to ground the guardianship of the truth of beyng.

The human (owned) in being appropriated, and indeed as *Da-sein.*

The latter already, because of the opening of appropriation, *historical.*

Why do we speak of a distinction? That is possible only if we compare the human as a being (in the metaphysical sense) with the rest. Yet does such a perspective still have legitimacy in beyng-historical terms? No; beyng-historically the human is the *drawn* one, that is, called in advance and attuned. This refers not to a comparing, but to the manner of his essencing.

## 111. Beyng

to be opened in thought. The strife of world toward earth in the crossing of its orbit through the countering of the god toward the human. This, however, is the carrying out of sustainment that is counterturning in itself as the commencement of the opening of appropriation.

Freeing into the succinctness of the owned.

## 112. The Owned

What becomes of *beings*, if they must manifest themselves within the grounded truth of beyng?

How shall we name beings, when they are no longer thought in terms of beingness and πρᾶγμα, *res*, thing, *ens creatum, objectum*, object . . . have become empty names?

Is the word of the being of beings now pronounced the *owned?* The eventful appropriating of the There and whatever is assigned to the latter itself, to the in-between of sustainment. Belonging in its own way in each case and at once to earth and world, to the human and the god.

The owned demands from us beforehand a wealth of instantiated ability to dispose over what is *peculiarly own*. Wealth is here not a consequence of possessing what is owned, but rather the ground for being capable of a renunciative disposing. "Renunciation" here is not rejection, but honoring that preserves, preserving in the reaches of the in-between.

*

The eventful appropriating of the There through the voice of silence, as clearing, at the same time lets earth find its way to world, the world to the human, the human to the god, and the god to the earth. This letting them find their way, as the essencing of beyng, grounds the owned and lets what is properly own emerge for it. It is not that the tree over there has its "particulars" for representational comparison and its "singular" status by virtue of its being there and now; it is not this that gives it peculiar ownness. Rather: earth closes itself within it, taking it into herself from its very roots, while the tree at the same time stands freely in the sphere of cleared references of worldly prevailing. It is *peculiarly its own* because it is grounded in a belonging to the in-between, so that, in each case differently, *it is an essential presence [Wesen] within the event of appropriation.*

*

We can employ the word like a name that names nothing, or that designates for us what has gone before, only in a different and arbitrary way.

Or the word can recollect us in [*uns er-innern*], into the "in-between" of the event of appropriation and can "say" to us and "ask" us whether we have forgotten beyng and merely set it aside at times like an empty husk that beings no longer need?

The word can transpose us into a history. In the time-space of such history, what is without decision becomes manifest to us—the undecidedness of the realm of all decisions, and thus also of all excuses and veilings.

The word can meaningfully point out to us the belonging of beings to beyng in such a manner that the latter is not a present ground that receives and contains, but rather that which first breaks apart beings to themselves and lets them essence in its (beyng's) clearing.

# The History of Beyng. Part II

*(The history of beyng* in the first word of beyng;
the word itself configured beyng-historically in the saying,
and only thus appropriated and in beyng.)

# XI. The Configuration of Saying

## 113. Beyng

is not something "living" ("vital"),
is not something "spiritual,"
is not something "material,"
is not something "immaterial."

For in all of these a relation to something that "is" is assumed, starting from which beyng is explained and interpreted.

The simple step must be taken: That beyng is *not* something that is, *not* a being.

Beyng is beyng (un-concealing—event).

Yet how is this, that is, its pure essencing, to be known?

The fact that in each case being is explained in terms of beings, and on what grounds this happens—to demonstrate this entails the overcoming of metaphysics from out of beyng itself. You may no longer evade by taking refuge in "beings," and the "distinction" is not something indifferent. And even the distinction must be said only *by way of transition,* so as to be *abandoned* in the readying of the other commencement. (Cf. Overcoming of Metaphysics, II. Continuation.[1]) The recovery of beyng.

## 114. The History of Beyng[2]

Resonance (of eventful appropriation, over everything to follow, attuning it).

Interplay (of the first commencement in terms of history as essencing of the truth of beings as such as a whole). Metaphysics as essential ground of Western history. Beginning (Plato—Aristotle), turning (Descartes—Leibniz) and consummation (Hegel—Nietzsche).

Leap (out of the arc of the thrownness of Da-sein (not "of the human being") through eventful appropriation).

---

1. Cf. "The Overcoming of Metaphysics." In: *Metaphysics and Nihilism.* Gesamtausgabe vol. 67.

2. Cf. *Contributions to Philosophy (Of the Event).* Gesamtausgabe vol. 65.

| | |
|---|---|
| Grounding | (of the abyssal ground of the in-between as that of the truth of beyng). Da-sein appropriated in the appropriative event. |
| Those who steadfastly insist | (the first guardians of Da-sein. Not yet its grounders). |
| The last god | (the inceptual one in the essencing of beyng, for its appropriation, unconcerned about the human being). |

A god who would like to raise himself beyond being, or indeed is thus raised and made into the source (cause) of being (not simply of beings) *"is"* no god and can *be* no god.

More inceptual than *every* god is beyng.

## 115. *The History of Beyng*

The first commencement is φύσις itself.

"Being" is not distinguished from truth. Both "are" the Same, which is also why the essential saying of Parmenides is immediately said: τὸ γὰρ αὐτὸ νοεῖν ἐστίν τε καὶ εἶναι.

Being is not distinguished or differentiated from the "becoming" that is seen by Parmenides and Heraclitus in terms of the essence of φύσις and said in different ways. For both, φύσις is λόγος.

In that φύσις is said each time as νοεῖν—λόγος, εἶναι too and ἀλήθεια first come into their own clearing and into the possibility of separation. Thereby *at the same time* δόξα, "appearing," as the essencing of φύσις—ἀλήθεια.

How in general the εἶδος becomes essential for "being," and that is, for revealing, over δόξα in the dual sense of appearing (shining and merely seeming so). Whence δόξα?

How, with the interpretation of the εἶδος as ἰδέα, being itself becomes ὄντως ὄν and distinguished against μὴ ὄντα (εἴδωλα).

Here lies the prefiguring of being for objectivity (in the modern sense).

With the grasping of the εἶδος, φύσις, and together with it ἀλήθεια, has receded back into the commencement and become unattainable. Νοεῖν and λέγειν themselves are torn away from φύσις and made the responsibility of the human; the human being himself now receives his essence as ζῷον λόγον ἔχον.

## 115. The History of Beyng [133–134]

Λόγος—νοῦς—διανοεῖσθαι—ἀπόφανσις—ἀπόφασις "λέγειν" now already become that which stands opposite to "beings," although not yet as "Subject" (truth as ὀρθότης and ὁμοίωσις).

Nowhere, admittedly, do Plato or Aristotle explain being in terms of beings. Yet this holding fast to being as that which is distinguished from beings indeed compels at the same time an appeal to ἰδεῖν ("ideas") and to κατηγορεῖσθαι ("categories"). Being becomes the apriori.

Metaphysics has begun: being as the beingness of beings has precedence in relation to beings and becomes the responsibility of *"ratio,"* the intellect and the will, of God, of *justitia*.

The change from correctness (ὀρθότης—ὁμοίωσις) to *certitudo* brings the determination of the essence of being as *repraesentatio* ("subjectivity"). All that now remains is: The unfolding of representation into the unconditional character of "thinking" (as absolute Spirit) and/or the unfolding of the human into the "over-man." In each instance an ultimate refuge is taken in "activity," be it that of reason thinking itself or that of the will as will to power.

The fading and mixing of the two into the mere "activity" of an indeterminate "dynamism" is already a decline within this final position of consummated metaphysics. *Actus purus* as paradigm for "actualism."

In contrast to metaphysics and its history, and thus also in a decisive break with all metaphysical interpretation on the part of Western philosophy as a whole, including, therefore, its commencement, *Being and Time* commences the other commencement in preparing the question of being.

Not only is truth experienced as a revealing, and not only is this experienced as the essencing of beyng itself, but over and beyond the first commencement, beyng becomes truth in its essencing, for which it demands grounding from out of itself, that is, from out of its *more inceptual* essence. Thus the event of beyng appropriates Da-sein.

*Da-sein* is not νοῦς and is not ψυχή, is not the human being and is not "consciousness," is not "Subject," and is not Spirit, and is not "practical life."

Da-sein is the essencing of revealing and demands an inceptual finding of the essence of the human being in terms of his relation to the truth of beyng (not only to the truth of beings). The human essence is eventfully appropriated into Da-sein and grounded.

Yet initially, in the transition from the first to the other commencement, when the entire tradition of metaphysics and the purely metaphysical interpretation on the part of all philosophy dominates everything, everything is ambiguous and nowhere is there a pure finding or unambiguous saying, nowhere the inceptual opening and cultivation of the essencing of beyng into its word. And yet everywhere the decisive stance of inceptual knowing and an impotence with regard to the inevitable metaphysical misinterpretation.

Beyng is the appropriative event. It has no ground, for it *is* the essential, abyssal ground of the *in-between* of the happening of appropriation. This saying also no longer holds itself within opposition; rather, the word is delivered over and answers to beyng and belongs to it alone.

Da-sein must *find* its way into beyng and leave history to beyng.

Beyng in its dignity does not require domination.

The first commencement has become more inceptual and more primary, and for this very reason, beyng no longer essences as φύσις. Above all, "metaphysics" is without soil or ground. Yet for this reason, its progeny dominates: *the worldview.*

\*

Which is more essential: to commence the other commencement, or to supposedly already go beyond it in turn and abandon it? Which beginning, however, is determined by a commencement cannot be known.

### 116. *The History of Beyng*

To say what is inceptual, and to say it *in such a way* that a reserving of silence concerning that which keeps itself silent (beyng) is eventfully appropriated by the latter. Whether it is, the guardians know not.

To say what is inceptual, so that within the first commencement the other one commences. Not a matter of historiographically ascertaining the "other commencement," of announcing it or even discussing it.

In its saying, knowing always errs prematurely into the realm of contrivance, and can only on few occasions bring the essencing of truth into the shelter of the long commencement.

The commencement is in-finite, that is, essentially longer than every open and opened up "history" proceeding from it as a sequence of occurrences.

The haste of things should never make the guardians over-hasty and force them into impatience.

For this too they must forego in advance: the pressure to effect a historiographically noticeable beginning through the precipitous reversal of what was already uprooted early on (metaphysics). To be "new" is the business of those who never experience the old, because they are excluded from the commencement.

Yet in the abandonment of beings by beyng through their being unleashed into self-blinding machination, the concealing of beyng appears; not beyng itself indeed, but the beckoning that goes through an ungrounded and unfathomable open, which is the sustainment itself.

## 117. *The History of Beyng*

meaning: the history whose essence beyng itself "is." Not the "history" that beyng passes through, not the "history" that can be recorded from it, nor indeed recorded as a sequence of opinions "about" being.

The history of beyng is the essence of beyng, but essence is essencing, and the latter is what history is, in the manner of commencing.

History is therefore on each and every occasion the history "of" the commencement. It is always that which is inceptual and within the inceptual.

History can never be experienced "historiographically," still less "thought" in such a way.

The commencement is to be thought only in an inceptual manner, going back into it, and from out of *such* concealing as its provenance.

The commencement is that which determines future history in such a way that in the other commencement, it grounds itself in the open (it is not replaced by the other commencement, for instance), or that each and every thing that is inceptual completely recedes into itself and beings only drain off into mere historiographical technicity *without history.*

The commencement, of such an essence, is that which determines the history on whose periphery a few of those who are to come may perhaps think the era: the age of the time—how close it is to the commencement and how remote.

*The era,* the present one in its essence, not the historiographically calculated "period," is the arrival of the commencement as being's abandonment. The latter is supreme concealing, and indeed at the same time to the point of unrecognizability, through the admittance of machination.

## 118. *Beyng*

All "beings" and their "being" (beingness) are beyngs "of" beyng: appropriated from out of beyng into its clearing.

Beyng can never be attained starting from beyngs. This, admittedly, is what the truth of beings as such as a whole wants. Here, beings are already set apart in the distinction, and being is contrasted with them as *their* beingness, albeit set over them.

The being of beings (already the admittance of (beyngs), that are of (beyng)), projected starting from beings, only comes back to the latter and remains within this span.

Here being then becomes divine, or belongs to humankind (in modernity), or angelic. Here it is ambassador, something made, it is a makeshift, and always cast down to the slave of beings.

The priority of beings before being, which as the "apriori" (sprung from what came forth before and become what merely goes before) remains a supplement, brings the truth of beings into the essence of the truth of beings as such beings and as a whole. Both—beings as such beings (ᾗ; *qua*) and the whole—are enjoined to being proceeding from beings.

Yet what is the ground of the truth of beings as ἰδέα?

What is the ground for locating and preserving the ἰδέα *and* ἐνέργεια within the creator God (who sets forth in representational setting-before)?

What is the ground for accommodating the ἰδέα and ἐνέργεια, the *ideae* and the *actus*, in representational setting-before, which as representational being set before, itself acting and striving and "active," becomes recast into objectivity, and the latter into beingness in the sense of secureness and certainty?

What is the ground for this transformation of truth into the certainty of representing-striving beings, of being as subjectivity initially still conditioned by things, conditioned only insofar as not yet fully comprehended in its essencing and calculated in terms of its accessibility for the human being as researcher (science of nature in Kant)? Whence the finitude of being, which thus is, after all, only an obstacle for the essence of subjectivity, which in itself is unconditional. (This finitude falsely brought together with the essence of beyng, which is indeed neither divine, nor human, nor angelic.)

What is the ground for the transformation from conditioned subjectivity to unconditional subjectivity?

What is the ground for unconditional subjectivity turning around in the leap into consummated subjectivity?

Wherein does consummation occur, and what is it?

On each occasion and in a different way each time, far out into its essence, the happening of appropriation is decisive here, as the unleashing of being into beingness.

Its essential consequence in the configuring and instituting of the truth of beings as such as a whole (metaphysics) is the oblivion of being in favor of the precedence of beings.

Supreme oblivion, when "being" and "becoming" have become "values," that is, machinating conditions of the supreme will to power.

On each occasion and for a long time thereafter, only occurrences and "histories" and dealings and "accomplishments" and "rescues" are admitted within such "truth," and everywhere there is a cheerful and irksome oblivion in pursuing what is current. This, however, belongs already to the domain of vacuous publicness, which, as a consequence of the historical human being's belonging to the truth of beyng, is admittedly not a matter of indifference.

## 119. Beyng[3]

The emptiest and the wealth.
The most universal and the singular.
The most understandable and the concealing.
The most used and that which springs forth.
The most reliable and the abyssal ground.
The most forgotten and the inner recollection (those who inwardly recollect).
The most said and the keeping silent.
The most arbitrary and the uncircumventable.
The afterword and naming word for the "is" of the assertion and the foreword and time-word for the ground of keeping silent.

It is not opposites of equal rank that are represented before us here for comparison; rather, the essencing of being itself is named. What looks like "opposite" is the intimacy of unleashing into beingness as refusal, is concealing within the happening of appropriation, is: the event of appropriation.

(Cf. second trimester, 1940, last part, in the form of a didactic hint; no suitable word.[4])

Nor is what is "opposite" sublated into some "third," rather, what might seem thus is that which is inceptual, concealing, keeping silent as the rising attuning of clearing, and thus of the There, and thus of Da-sein, and thus the *possibility* of those who steadfastly insist, and

---

3. Cf. *Grundbegriffe*. Freiburg lecture course of summer semester 1941. Gesamtausgabe vol. 51. Edited by Petra Jaeger. Frankfurt am Main: Vittorio Klostermann, 1981. Translated as *Basic Concepts* by Gary E. Aylesworth. Bloomington: Indiana University Press, 1993.

4. Cf. *Nietzsche: European Nihilism*. Freiburg lecture course, second trimester 1940. Gesamtausgabe vol. 48. Edited by Petra Jaeger. Frankfurt am Main: Vittorio Klostermann, 1986, 322ff.

thus a few beyng-historical human beings, and thus perhaps—which is inessential in the face of beyng—an other humankind.

## 120. Beyng

is not an object and is nothing present at hand and nothing universal or merely encompassing, but ownmost in essence. Even our *relationship* to beyng belongs to beyng, and its essence must accordingly prevail; even our relationship to beyng is grounded in truth, which is *of* beyng, and the latter must also let this relationship spring forth within itself.

## 121. Guiding Words[5]

Being is the nothing.
The nothing nihilates.
The nihilating refuses (that beings can ever "be" from out of beings).
The refusal grants (the clearing, within which what we call beings can go in and out and presence from time to time).
The granting opens the appropriation of the in-between (of time-space).
The opening of appropriation is the suddenness of attuning.
The attuning is the first opening of silencing.
The opening of silencing is the inceptual word.
The word is beyng in its essencing.

## 122. Only Beyng Is

*Terrifying dis-placement* as one essencing of beyng.

*

*Steadfast in-sistence* as the essencing of Da-sein.

*

*Essencing* as the event of truth.

---

5. Cf. §44. "The Dis-tinction."

*

The *event* as beyng.
 *Beyng as truth.*
 *Only beyng is.*

## 123. Beyng

that originarily alienates itself from all power and never needs power;

that leaves every charming and imposing character of the "elemental" outside of it;

the pure dignity of the event of truth;

(truth, however, as clearing of self-concealing);

the stillness that all adventurers run up against and are thrust back into their dreams, so as to slurp up this fare in the manner of those who overplay with all the "refinements" of literary arts.

That which waits, which only ever approaches the opening of pure thinking, not to be tasted by the senses nor to be calculated by the intellect.

The event—before all gods and humans, animals, plants, and stones.

## 124. Beyng

not "becoming," not effecting, not making, not power, not mere constancy.

All of this is a semblance of beyng, a semblance permitted where beyng conceals itself and the ἰδέα is left to the mercy of the objectification that ensues.

*Beyng the revealing of concealing*, as the appropriative event of the clearing that calls to decision what we name the gods, what we are otherwise familiar with as the human being.

The revealing of concealing makes concealing manifest as such, but does not sublate it, for instance.

## 125. Beyng Is the Once[a]

That which essentially prevails in having been and coming at the same time—that which comes as the inceptual.

---

a. Ms.: *Once* [*einst*] = "previously" *and* "in future."

Beyng is "time."
The law of beyng: clearing of concealing. Passing into concealment as arising out of it.
Such is placed and enjoined by beyng. Beyng is this jointure.
Beyng is.
*This is the singular saga.*

\*

Beyng has never yet been enquired after at all, but only ever beings as such beings. And what they name "being" is meant as *beings as a whole* or their "universality."

Cf. Schelling's distinction between *"being and beings,"* "ground and existence," "basis" and that which exists.[6]

The ambiguity of the ὄν as *participium*.

In order to experience the *relation to being* purely, being must have oscillated over into its clearing, and the relation must go into this clearing, and from here determine and attune that which relates.

### 126. Event

The event comes to appropriate, appropriates to *itself*, to the buoyancy of the holy, to the human being steadfastly insistent within Da-sein (exposed to beyng as concealing).

*The happening of appropriation* and *steadfast insistence of Da-sein.*

Both first to be prepared in the transition as the overcoming of metaphysics.

The steadfast insistence of composure must first be struggled for and carried out wholly from out of this *between time*, and especially the ability to listen to the attuning voice of the word of beyng.

The other commencement is more inceptual than the first, and yet still and in this way related to it as the preceding one.

### 127. The Event of Appropriation and the History of Beyng

Only from out of the beyng-historical experience of beyng as event does the history of beyng allow itself to be experienced as instantiated in terms of the event.

---

[6]. Cf. *Schelling: On the Essence of Human Freedom (1809)*. Freiburg lecture course, summer semester 1936. Gesamtausgabe vol. 42. Edited by Ingrid Schüßler. Frankfurt am Main: Vittorio Klostermann, 1988.

Only thus can the history of metaphysics manifest itself as a species of the history of the truth of being, since metaphysics is the truth of beings.

Only thus does this history of metaphysics become withdrawn from objectification through a historiographical history of philosophy.

Only thus will the history of philosophy come to be taken back into itself from beyng in the manner of the event, and every essential questioning become truly historical: *Da-sein*.

## 128. In the Event of Appropriation

truth prevails in its essence, compelling the true within it, and grounding cognition and extending its tension into beings.

It is only ever from out of beyng that the relaxation of such tension in turn arises.

## 129. Truth as the Clearing

The open of the clearing is not some indeterminate emptiness into which something "appears."

The clearing is on each occasion configured in the manner of the event, and unfolded into projective realms and paths by the Da-sein that has been appropriated and steadfastly insists within it. All of this is determined from out of the truth of beyng and what is up for decision as this history.

Clearing from out of the event.

Unconcealment from out of arising (φύσις), presencing.

## 130. Truth

is in the founding of being (poetizing[b]), is in the grounding of beyng (thinking).

For truth is the clearing of beyng itself.

And it also springs forth from beyng itself.

So that everything rides on the fact that beyng is and beings "are" "not."

Yet in what way "is" beyng? *The event.*

---

b. Trs.: Knows nothing of beyng!

(When today one repeats "being is," one means "beings," or else one withdraws from reflection with the assurance, seemingly protecting the miraculous, that being does not let itself be "defined." As though beyng demanded a "definition.")

### 131. Concealing

From where does concealing stem?
How does concealing prevail in essence?
What is concealing?
It is beyng itself, which in clearing veils and cloaks itself, as clearing, precisely through those (beings) that come to presence. Everything thus depends on the clearing, that it come to be appropriated, that in the appropriative event a "that" (that beyng is) first ground itself in its own and yet alienate everything that is capable of coming to presence into the clearing.

### 132. Truth

So long as we think "truth" in the conventional metaphysical way, it is always "truth about . . ."—and secondary and supplemental.
If, however, its essence is recognized as clearing, then the truth "of" beyng is not "truth about . . . ," but beyng itself, and indeed in its essencing.
To enquire concerning the "meaning of being" does not mean to erect statements "about" being and to ponder and report these statements as doctrines, but rather to open, in thinking, our relation to beyng itself. "Time" is the last foreword of the word of being. The "meaning of being" asks for the first time, in contrast to all metaphysics, concerning beyng itself, and in a manner more inceptual than the first commencement.

### 133. Is Beyng Always?

Beyng is neither "always" (*sempiternum*), nor is it "eternal," nor is it "temporal," "for a time," from time to time.
When and how long being "is" cannot be asked. Such a question passes "by" beyng in its questioning.

## 134. Beyng as Event of Appropriation

attunes and appropriates "thinking" to itself. The latter is opened and seized by beyng.

Every beyng-historical concept is a *being opened and seized*. *Opening seizure and attunement.*

# XII. The History of Beyng
## (Da-sein)

### 135. Da-sein

Reserving essence and word for the interval, first to be cleared in its essence, of the Between between beyng and human.

### 136. That the Historical Human Being Comes into His Essence (Da-sein)

itself essential for "history" as decision of the essence of the truth of beyng.

That the human being become "essential" is here not meant in a "moral" sense, nor in an existentiell sense, nor "metaphysically," and especially not at all anthropologically.

### 137. Da-sein

is beyng-historical in essence, and therefore not to be demonstrated everywhere and at all times, for instance, thinking back to the history of metaphysics. It does not at all permit itself to be "pointed out."

Da-*sein* is the word for the grounding of the truth of beyng from out of beyng as the attuning determination of the essence of "ground," and all this is in turn already essencing of beyng.

### 138. Protection

Protection in awaiting beyng.
  Preserving the *disconcerting*, being capable of it.
  Only thus being *appropriated over* into beyng.
  The disconcerting now a "being," without beyng.
  (Beyng) concealing.

### 139. Errancy

not as a mistake or error in thinking and representing the already secured domain of objects that stand over against us.

Not "guilt" or "inability," rather their ground is the originary, inceptual concealing, into whose domains knowledge does not reach, because it is excluded from the clearing from out of beyng by beyng.

*Errancy* belongs to the There [Da-] of Da-sein. Steadfast insistence within the There then indeed essentially unfolds the being appropriated over into concealing that has occurred.

Within errancy itself, closing off clears itself in a concealed manner; and through it, essentially, is a world.

### 140. Da-sein

names the site and gathered traits of the human's being appropriated in the fundamental trait of his being drawn to beyng.

The essence of Da-sein is *steadfast insistence* (care).

Steadfastly in-sistent in the realm of the owned, that is, in its essence (guardianship of the truth of beyng), appropriated over to it.

*Da-sein* is the between-ground, appropriated from out of beyng, between beyng and the human. Da-sein "carries" the abyss of ground. Thinking the essence of the human from out of Da-sein (*never* again: neither as spirit, nor as reason—nor as "body").

Thought *thus*, the human being is "conceived" in terms of the no longer conceived essence of beyng and of truth (of buried φύσις and ἀλήθεια), an essence already veiled in the commencement.

### 141. Being's Abandonment

Being everywhere abandons beings, leaving them to the claws and talons of objectification. The objective is the spoils of calculation. Objectivity poses itself in the place of being. "Beings" disintegrate. And being has concealed itself.

And nevertheless the din and rush of everything imposes itself and denies what has gone before and disseminates the semblance of the new.

Not a trace leading to being remains anywhere, for even beings have been eroded by use into calculated contrivance. The latter lays claim to all passion and every meaning.

Everything becomes ever more new and ever more rapidly new. Unconditional planning secures for what is objective the possibility of the most constant and rapid alternation; what is without substance is what endures and has its presencing in the shining of mere semblance. The unconditional character of the shining of mere semblance demands of everyone who does not want to perish here that they "engage" in this process. The shining semblance itself, however, is incapable of acknowledging itself, since before all else it must first of all constantly evade itself so as not to discover what is behind it. Shining semblance must continually keep itself on track and divert calculation and suffering onto the objective.

If, however, someone were capable of recognizing shining semblance in its essencing and of grounding an open for this shining, then such shining and semblance would reveal itself as beyng that recedes into concealing.

### 142. The Projections of the Being of Beings from Out of the Casting of Being Itself[1]

That, as a consequence of metaphysics and of the interpretation of the same as culture and human achievement, we regard the being of beings in each case as a figment of thought and concept and opinion and doctrine.

Only from out of the overcoming of metaphysics do we experience being—as that which essences as the truth of beings and as the concealing of itself.

Only steadfast insistence within the history of beyng overcomes the historiographical manner of thinking that bundles together everything that belongs within the same *not* knowing itself and rejects all comparison if such comparing wants more than to know what is trivial and incomparable.

### 143. Seeking More Essentially the Other Commencement

Not determining differently, for instance, something given, handed down, (art, gods, knowledge, history, humankind, truth), expressing a new view, but rather putting all this in question.

Making worthy of question not as "thematic" objects but from afar as unnamed, from out of other, more essential decisions. Cf. on overcoming: On the Origin of the Work of Art.[2]

We should not *bundle together* via historiography what in each case, from out of its ownmost commencement, after all belongs to itself in a concealed manner in the same *not* knowing of itself and prevails in essence from out of this belonging to itself.

---

1. Cf. "The Overcoming of Metaphysics." In: *Metaphysics and Nihilism.* Gesamtausgabe vol. 67.
2. "The Origin of the Work of Art." In: *Holzwege.* Gesamtausgabe vol 5. Edited by F.-W. von Herrmann. Frankfurt am Main: Vittorio Klostermann, 1977, 1–74.

### 144. Word and Language[a]

Language has become a means of transport, like the motor vehicle it serves only transportation and is otherwise nothing.

Language is a tool for inculcating scarcely pondered opinions of the days that come and go and their daily character, opinions that are not even believed.

Language no longer has anything of the essence of the word, it has almost lost even its corrupted essence.

Nor will it win it back through a "cultivation" of language. For in this way too, and with complete finality, its origin from the word is buried.

The word is clearing of the stillness of beyng.

All affectations of the writers of set script and initiates of script remain only ultimate stray paths belonging to a blind urge.

### 145. The Decision

not Christendom, not morality, not factual needs and interests of life, not justification of the "enemy," nor even feelings directed back at one's "own"—none of these are standards by which to indicate the realm of the decision.

For everywhere yet everything remains contorted into power, and that means into the precedence of beings through beingness as machination.

How small and desolate everything remains, dragging itself down to the lowest realm of opposition, and more desolate still through the seemingly noble appeal to "reason."

Yet what does "reason" mean here?

Where is there here even a single step or a slightest beckoning of being?

Where an essential elevation beyond the enemy?

Everywhere enslavement to its worst and what is shouted out as worst.

Racial salvation and protection of freedom are on reciprocally opposing sides the walls of pretext behind which pure power exerts itself.

---

a. Ms.: Being's abandonment.

## 146. Beyng

appropriates beings into the event of appropriation (the essencing of truth).

## 147. The History of Beyng

The first commencement is essencing of φύσις as ἀλήθεια. *One* essential and prevailing way in which humankind is drawn into a relation to beyng and from *there,* out of this inceptuality, the originary character of a historical effecting of the gods.

The first end is already determined in its beginning by the beginning of metaphysics in which beginning being is interpreted as ἰδέα.

The end is consummated in the destruction of the essence of truth, a truth that has meanwhile declined, because it remained ungroundable.

This destruction is being's abandonment of beings in the form of the power of machination. Forgotten and nihilative the belonging to being.

## 148. The History of the Human in Being

How through the truth of being the human being is relinquished to himself, namely, into the *semblance that is subjectivity.* "Semblance" is ambiguous: the *appearing* of beings in the light of their being represented before us, so that the human being has the semblance of being producer and owner and this semblance what is properly real, true to reality—"life."

In truth, that is, in the truth of beyng, however?

How here the essencing of beyng first brings itself into its light?

## 149. History

To what extent, and for what reason, it occurs in multiple realms and "grounds," fore- and backgrounds at once, and indeed necessarily so.

1. the catchwords, public opinion, "slogans" ("plutocracy," "freedom").

2. the goals and intents that are posited on each occasion, but not said.
3. the "forces" and powers that can be directly experienced in the public realm.
4. the concealed essence of being that makes the pushers and actors into the pushed and abandoned slaves.

All to be known at once. And each in its uncircumventable character.

### 150. Democritus, Fragment 269

τόλμα πρήξιος ἀρχή,
τύχη δὲ τέλεος κυρίη.[3]

Risk is the commencement of action,
Destiny, however, mistress of the end.

τύχη: reaching, apportioning, *summoning*—(event).
(How far is beyng summoning in advance?)

### 151. The Thinker

The thinker amid beings remains exposed to beyng.
　The others "commit themselves" to beings amid beings.

### 152. They Rail Surreptitiously and Openly . . .

They rail surreptitiously and openly against philosophy made of "words" and have no intimation of how they contest their sham philosophy exclusively by taking refuge in the discourse of "subject" and "object," of "meaning" and "conferral of meaning," etc. They are of the opinion that if they do *not* ponder the dubious provenance of their basic concepts, their thinking is already a thinking in terms of the "matter."
　The pitiful wretches and their vanity!

---

3. Cf. Hermann Diels, *Die Fragmente der Vorsokratiker*. Edited by Walther Kranz. Volume Two. 5th edition. Berlin: Weidmannsche Buchhandlung, 1935, B 269.

## 153. History, Commencement, Downgoing

All beginning, the more genuinely it becomes a beginning, is destined for downgoing in that which comes to the fore as its consummation.

Only the commencement eludes the downgoing. Beginning, however, is not commencement.

What is commencement?

## 154. "Ego" and "Subject"

If the Ego (e.g., the ἐγώ of Protagoras and of the Greeks generally) is not "Subject" in the Cartesian sense, then this at the same time says: to the essence of subjectivity there does not also belong I-ness.

## 155. The Being of Beings and Beyngs of Beyng

The being of beings and beyngs of beyng.

Between them, by virtue of they themselves, the abyssal ground of commencements.

The leap through the abyssal ground has been taken.

## 156. The History of Beyng

Important to show the *procedure of beyng-historical thinking in itself.*

For this the contrast with Hegel is appropriate, within certain limits: dialectical sublation into the unconditional. The contrast with Nietzsche: nihilistic inversion.

Yet because both are essential within *metaphysics,* and beyng-historical thinking out of the other commencement, the contrasting immediately—like every contrasting, yet here especially—becomes inappropriate, to the extent that it forces us back into the metaphysical and *in this way* works against itself.

The critical setting apart—contra-diction—the freeing of the commencement.

## 157. Experience and Steadfast Insistence

Yet does not every experience "of" beyng distort the latter into a being, and does it not demand that what is experienced be graspable and at our disposal?

Experience is here intended in the sense of instantiation, and, measured by every being, whether traditional or newly procured, what it experiences remains a nothing.

And this is why, faced with all that belongs to machination, steadfast insistence so readily disintegrates into what is "nihilative."

## 158. The Leap Off

Truth as the essencing of beyng from out of beyng, to be fathomed in grounding.

Fathoming the ground as steadfast insistence within Da-sein.

Steadfast insistence as belonging to concealing.

Fathoming the ground begins as questioning after, which can no longer be overthrowing, but comes from the *leap off*.

Yet nevertheless gathering of what essentially prevails in having been into the *one* prevailing in essence in the leap off.

Mere passing by is never liberation to freedom, the latter is: freedom for ground, whence the necessity of abyssal ground.

## 159. The First Commencement[4]

Being itself—φύσις—is the first commencement. And this commencement arises, is the arising of self-revealing emergence into its clearing through it at the same time essentially taking itself back into itself and refusing the grounding of unconcealment and abandoning itself to beingness. Here, the placing itself back into what is concealed, concealing, is what is essential, nothing negative!, rather *being a ground* itself!

Thus philosophy must then essentially take over the ungrounding, without knowing it; the essential and necessary de-fault in the grounding of ἀλήθεια.

De-fault—not failure, rather defaulting and taking up residence in the First, the fact that being appears at all and *is* the appearing. Having defaulted, philosophy is justified in its first work, and from this work becomes the configuring of the truth of beings as such as a whole, becomes metaphysics. Ἰδέα is especially a saving of φύσις—emergent appearing rising into the open of constant presencing—οὐσία—yet at

---

4. Cf. second trimester, 1940. On the Apriori. In: *Nietzsche: European Nihilism*. Freiburg lecture course. Gesamtausgabe vol. 48.

the same time it lays claim to ἰδεῖν, to νοεῖν as ἰδεῖν and distinguished from διανοεῖσθαι, that is, starting from the latter, that is, already from the priority of "beings."

The relation to being is not grounded in the unconcealment of φύσις (τὸ αὐτό) but on being as ἰδέα in *forgetting* already ἀλήθεια. Νοῦς and λόγος becomes the human capability to apprehend and discern the ideas.

Now *the relationship of the human being to being* is indeed necessarily retained, but ungrounded and therefore made into an endowment of the human being, and for this reason ultimately explicable in terms of the human, perhaps still in such a way that one lets this human being, thus endowed, have been created by a god who first drew the "ideas" into himself as what *he* represented before him, thus depriving them of their essence.

The first metaphysical, yet still concealed beginning of modern *subjectivity* is already found in the Christian, Augustinian interpretation of the ideas; indeed earlier still in the Hellenistic, Roman "Stoic" distortion of the entire truth of Greek "being."

Since then, the human being is indeed specifically in a relationship to being (beingness, "ideas," values), yet for this reason precisely ground-less. He is "animal"—and the consummate animal—as overman. Elimination, therefore, of the "human being" as *animal rationale*. All anthropology, however, the personified lack of commencement in philosophy, concerns itself with the opposite.

### 160. The Essencing of Truth as Clearing of Beyng

occurs on this side, and always outside, of the domain of the truth of beings as such as a whole, whether such beings are interpreted along the guiding thread of representational setting-before (thinking) or that of "bodying forth" (machinative calculation as thinking).

Where does truth prevail in essence?

Essentially to be experienced only out of the other commencement and as the other commencement.

The beyng-historical Where of abyssal ground.

### 161. The Human Being and Anthropology

When the human being lets knowledge concerning his essence become acquaintance with his qualities and finds satisfaction in anthropology.

This is no mere incapacity to think but oblivion of being, and the latter is being's abandonment.

### 162. *The Human*—animal rationale

From where does this experience of the essence of the human arise? Metaphysically:

1. Living being—φύσει—*a being that is,*
2. but λόγος—νοῦς.

*Relation to beings as such as a whole* therefore not (1) "biological," thus not (2) psychological—determined by a higher capability.

Cf. Aristotle, *Metaphysics* A1. Here the metaphysical ground for the fact that all anthropology, which essentially thinks in this way, remains excluded from metaphysics and especially from every philosophy. And perhaps wants to be excluded—out of anxiety in the face of being.

### 163. *Metaphysics—Anthropology*

What metaphysics can fundamentally never comprehend, the essence of reason, is demoted just as uncomprehendingly—by the overman—and replaced by the body.

Blindness *once again* and definitively. But now in the definitive semblance of what can be understood by everyone.

From "life" everything can be explained and everything conceived as its manifestation.

Just as geography can become a fundamental science, insofar as everything there is appears on earth.

### 164. *The First Commencement and the Human as* ζῷον λόγον ἔχον

In the history of the first commencement historical human beings default in the face of being, and being becomes for them an abode and even what is most in being.

At the same time, however, they necessarily become hasty, bringing themselves as "possessors" of νοῦς and λόγος into a relationship with "beings," yet without grounding precisely this relationship in its essential ground and determining their own human essence from out of this ground.

Ever since, the oblivion of being has begun.

Its history is the history of the truth of beings as metaphysics.

Yet this is not "decline" and the like, but the *first commencement*, that is, the history of the preparation of the other commencement, and that means, in turn, only of *commencement!*

## 165. The History of Essential Thinking

The history of essential thinking is the concealed event of the unspoken offsetting from one another of the projections of being upon its ungrounded essencing, through which offsetting each projection is in each case thrown into being and sheltered in being's truth.

The history of essential thinking is a history of being.

Essential thinking is image-less poetizing in the word of the saga of beyng.

## 166. Truth and Beyng
## The Essence of History

Truth, in its veiled and ungrounded essence, is the revealing "of" that which is self-concealing. As revealing, it is on each occasion a clearing of beings. With this clearing, therefore, because beings are opened up as such and as a whole through it and this opening happens, in each case in accordance with the brightness of the clearing and with the entry of beings into it as thus determined, a decision "about" beings is in each case attained in its essence: the de-cision here is that separating of the truth of beings from essential possibilities held in reserve and sanctioned, yet in each case not fulfilled now. The separating springs from and wrests itself free from the revealing "of" that which is self-concealing. This decision is what is essentially happening, the first and also last that is happening in essence, the fundamental trait of happening—and thus the lighting up of the essence of history.

Conceived from the perspective of this happening, and not in a still more originary way, the essence of history is that unconcealment of beings—and that means, as such and as a whole—"*is*." Being is essencing of revealing. This unconcealment (truth) does not first "have" a "history" in the sense of its own changing course in the sequence of time; it is of the essence of history, and therefore the ground of the history of "becoming" that alone is initially experienced (the arising and passing away of deeds, achievements, occurrences). The fact that it can still become the "object" of explanatory and interpretive inquiry at all (that there is historiography) is not grounded solely in the fact that there must be history, but that with history as the essencing of truth itself, a possible realm of clearing is made available for historiography as "opening up" and representational setting-before.

The revealing of beings as such as a whole, truth as prevailing in essence, because it is de-cision, in each case posits for itself the domain from which it at the same time comes to stand over against that "upon which" it has stumbled. It unveils its future to that which has been, first opened through that revealing itself, and its provenance for that which it must run up against, that which is coming.

It itself is the "coming," thought not in terms of temporal sequence, but as essencing of the happening of appropriation, standing in which Da-sein is appropriated into the appropriative event. The "coming" does not "come" from out of the "future" but rather first grounds it.

The "between" between the commencements.

## XIII. Beyng-Historical Thinking

## 167. Beyng-Historical Thinking and Philosophy

Only out of its relation to the first commencement, indeed, only out of its relation to what, as metaphysics, became the consequence of the first commencement, can inceptual thinking be named *philosophy*.

In truth, beyng-historical thinking is no longer and no more "philosophy." This truth must be taken seriously, with all its consequences; by doing so, the roots of all misplaced demands and efforts have also at once been torn out.

Why, and to what extent, does the end of art simultaneously coincide with the end of philosophy?

Certainly neither of the two ends ever decides of its own accord concerning the other commencement, nor above all concerning whether and to what extent the human being is appropriated into it. Thus everything remains ambiguous, and the effluents of metaphysics will lie for a long time over the open plain that has been devastated and even give rise to the illusion that they are the "rivers."

## 168. Beyng-Historical Thinking

stands outside of every relation to sciences, art, politics—that is, outside of what institutes itself as "culture," that is, the technicity of humankind become Subject, and decides in advance concerning beings. This, moreover, is all already prefigured in Plato's thinking, which begins metaphysics.

Beyng-historical thinking enquires concerning the decision of the essence of truth as the truth of beyng. This thinking thinks ahead into beyng and is in everything determined by beyng as that which singularly attunes it. Whether "sciences," "art," "politics" ever again become essential in the configuring of Dasein and from out of such configuring is not only questionable but fundamentally decided. To the effect that they can no longer be such.

## 169. "Philosophy" in the Other Commencement

The philosophy of the commencement, essential thinking, does not think the "human" and does not think the god, does not think the world and does not think the earth, does not think beings as such, does not think beings as a whole—but rather thinks: *beyng*.

Beyng, pondered in terms of all of the above, can never be grasped.
The first leap of thinking thinks:
Beyng is the nothing.
The nothing nihilates.
Nihilation refuses every explanation of beings in terms of beings.

Refusal, however, grants the clearing in which beings go in and out, and as such can be manifest and concealed.

The nothing displaces into terror. And this displacement into terror, from out of beings and away from any appeal to them, is the inceptual attuning through which the human being (and the gods) are *determinately attuned*.

Yet why are beings (metaphysics (faith, worldview)) still capable of standing in resistance to such terrifying displacement?

Do they stand in resistance to it?

And can the displacement into terror attune, so long as, following an uncircumventable, yet always misinterpretable hint concerning "attunement," we continue to persist in seeking in such "attunement" an object for "analyses" and anthropological findings?

### 170. "Philosophy"

The essential ambiguity in which "philosophy" now stands.

One can *reject* philosophy, because one regards it as superfluous, since solely the pursuit of beings now guides all need and all "attunement." The being of beings has been decided, so much so that this decision is no longer pondered at all any more.

On the basis of the unconditional oblivion of being and by virtue of "proximity" to the real, philosophy is consequently rejected and at most still disparaged. This stance indeed has greater historical force and insight than any scholarly obsession or apprehensiveness that would seek to "save" the "spiritual" by hanging on to a past that is barely comprehended any more.

\*

"Philosophy," however, must in truth be *overcome*, if its essence is metaphysics and all philosophy is conceived only metaphysically; striving for what is authentically knowable (as the "idea"); thus thought proceeding from beings and back to beings.

The overcoming of philosophy is separated by an abyss from its rejection, which after all precisely remains bound to it and makes a task out of oppositionality, and that means, makes philosophy into a "worldview." The latter, however, is only the corrupted essence of metaphysics. The overcoming is the essencing of beyng, rejection only a late consequence of the ever-uncomprehended machination, and thus merely something contrived.

### 171. The Commencement

as *self-concealing*, that which spreads strangeness and alienation around it; and enticing us, therefore, to also pass over it with the semblance of legitimacy, to let it sink away as something overcome that one will never again encounter.

Whereas the commencement is, after all, that which is coming.

### 172. Essential Thinking

*Circle* and *leap in*, in such a way that our full essence in advance is granted freedom and the subordination of thinking becomes necessary.

These two are precisely what is decisive and most difficult.

People are indeed of the opinion that making use of these errors and tricks is the easiest thing—as opposed to *exact* research!! and proceeding step by step!

In essential thinking there are no paths laid out in advance. Only where it travels *is* there a way, and its traveling opens the experiencing of beyng. And the way leaves scarcely a trace behind it.

### 173. Beyng-Historical Thinking

1. not description and demonstration,
2. not derivation from highest concepts,
3. rather, appropriated *saying* of the *appropriative happening* of history as *Da-sein*.
4. *the word* "of" beyng.
5. the beyng-historical genitive (*not* "objective" and "subjective" genitive).

### 174. Freedom

is belonging to the owned of beyng. The owned of beyng is truth essencing as the clearing of concealing.

*The binding from out of beyng that is not bound to beings.*
*Essential intimacy of truth and freedom.*

### 175. Honoring and Valuing[a]

Valuing is measuring and can also usurp honoring as the "valuing"—calculative settling—of a valuing.

*Honoring* itself experiences dignity, retains it, and does not debase itself to a valuing.

It *recognizes* the valuing of beings as a dishonoring of beyng.

Yet this recognition is at the same time a passing by (leap off), nothing on the basis of which dignity would bestow something on which it would support itself.

### 176. Questioning[1]

as questioning opening onto the truth of beyng, the sole way of honoring beyng.

Beyng as event.

### 177. Pure Finding

Creative finding is not thinking up, is not calculative figuring out, is not forcing, but rather finding one's way into the owned—coming to be that which is *appropriated.*

*Being determined through that which attunes.*

Without preemptive taking away in advance; without the going ahead of procedure.

Seeking on the basis of *pure finding.*

*Coming upon it.*

### 178. The Sequence of Publications
### (in short treatises)

1. *What Is Metaphysics?*[2]
   Fourth and expanded edition (another "talk" added).

---

a. Ms.: Overcoming of Metaphysics. Leaving dignity! Not *obsequiousness; questioning!*

1. Cf. foundational words.
2. In: *Wegmarken.* Gesamtausgabe vol. 9, 103–122.

2. *On the Essence of Truth*[3]
   1. The truth lecture of 1930, as revised in 1940.
   2. Unconcealment (ἀλήθεια—φύσις). Parmenides[4]—Heraclitus[5]—Anaximander.[6]
3. *The Consummation of Metaphysics*
   Nietzsche's metaphysics: Presentation (five foundational words).[7]
   Cf. *draft;* interpretation (unconditional and consummated *subjectivity*).
   Critical encounter (power—as machination, "power" and ἰδέα—ἀγαθόν, *machination* and *event*).
3a. *The transition of metaphysics into the corruption of its essence (the "worldview").*
4. *The Overcoming of Metaphysics*[8]
   1. The overcoming as history "of" beyng, not as something contrived by thinkers and human beings.
   2. Da-sein.
5. *The History of Beyng*
   Retain the draft of the *Contributions* for it as its innermost structure (cf. *The History of Beyng*[9]).
   *Contributions*[10] and *Mindfulness*[11] as preliminary works.
   (The *lecture courses* as "elucidations" coming from the outside in each case and assimilating to still current opinion. Their saying can never be accomplished from out of beyng, but rather only ever guides toward it. And thus within *their* purview what is essential is each time and necessarily obstructed and distorted in the very mention of it.)

---

3. In: *Wegmarken*. Gesamtausgabe vol. 9, 177–202.

4. Cf. *Parmenides*. Freiburg lecture course, winter semester 1942–43. Gesamtausgabe vol. 54. Edited by Manfred S. Frings. Frankfurt am Main: Vittorio Klostermann, 1982. Translated as *Parmenides* by André Schuwer and Richard Rojcewicz. Bloomington: Indiana University Press, 1992.

5. Cf. *Heraclitus*. Gesamtausgabe vol. 55.

6. Cf. "The Saying of Anaximander." In: *Holzwege*. Gesamtausgabe vol. 5, 321–376.

7. Cf. *Nietzsche's Metaphysics*. Freiburg lecture course of winter semester 1941–42, announced but not delivered. *Introduction to Philosophy—Thinking and Poetizing*. Freiburg lecture course, winter semester 1944–45. Gesamtausgabe vol. 50. Edited by Petra Jaeger. Frankfurt am Main: Vittorio Klostermann, 1990.

8. "The Overcoming of Metaphysics." In: *Metaphysics and Nihilism*. Gesamtausgabe vol. 67.

9. *The History of Beyng* (in this volume).

10. *Contributions to Philosophy (Of the Event)*. Gesamtausgabe vol. 65.

11. *Mindfulness*. Gesamtausgabe vol. 66.

## XIII. Beyng-Historical Thinking [173]

6. *Interpretations of Hölderlin*
   As when on a holiday[12]
   Ripe, bathed in fire . . .[13]
   Remembrance[14]
   Mnemosyne[15]
   The Rhine[16]
   Germania[16]

---

12. In: *Elucidations of Hölderlin's Poetry*. Gesamtausgabe vol. 4. Edited by F.-W. von Herrmann. Frankfurt am Main: Vittorio Klostermann, 1981, 49–78. Translated as *Elucidations of Hölderlin's Poetry* by Keith Hoeller. Amherst, NY: Humanity Books, 2000, 67–99.
13. Cf. "Remembrance." In: *Elucidations of Hölderlin's Poetry*. Gesamtausgabe vol. 4, 115f.; trans. 101f.
14. Cf. *Hölderlin's Hymn "Remembrance."* Freiburg lecture course, winter semester 1941–42. Gesamtausgabe vol. 52. Edited by Curd Ochwadt. Frankfurt am Main: Vittorio Klostermann, 1982.
15. Cf. *Hölderlin's Hymn "The Ister."* Freiburg lecture course, summer semester 1942. Gesamtausgabe vol. 53. Edited by Walter Biemel. Frankfurt am Main: Vittorio Klostermann, 1984, 184ff. Translated as *Hölderlin's Hymn "The Ister"* by William McNeill and Julia Davis. Bloomington: Indiana University Press, 1996. Also: "Hölderlin, Andenken und Mnemosyne." In: *Zu Hölderlin—Griechenlandreisen*. Gesamtausgabe vol. 75. Edited by Curd Ochwadt. Frankfurt am Main: Vittorio Klostermann, 2000.
16. Cf. *Hölderlins Hymnen "Germanien" und "Der Rhein."* Freiburg lecture course, winter semester 1934–35. Gesamtausgabe vol. 39. Edited by Susanne Ziegler. Frankfurt am Main: Vittorio Klostermann, 1980. Translated as *Hölderlin's Hymns "Germania" and "The Rhine"* by William McNeill and Julia Ireland. Bloomington: Indiana University Press, 2014.

# Κοινόν
## Out of the History of Beyng (1939–40)

Κοινόν
Out of the History of Beyng

## τὸ κοινόν. Out of the History of Beyng

Today, all experience everywhere, and are quick to note, what is "strange" about this second World War. Yet for many, the everydayness that grinds everything down has also already blurred this strangeness into something habitual. Others are of the opinion that the beginning of the hitherto typical actions of war must surely put an end to this strange state of affairs. Terrible things may then happen to people. Yet the definiteness of acting together gives as much as it takes, and eliminates the burdensome intangibility of the strange. Others again find this World War not at all "remarkable." They regard this "strangeness" as what is "normal" in what is now after all "modern" war, with a marked superciliousness that is nevertheless not entirely sure of itself. They persuade themselves, or even just repeat after others, that something that is affirmed as "modern" has also entered the realm of what is not strange and therefore unquestionable. Whoever "feels" something to be strange is indeed judging from the perspective of what is habitual for him. If he remains at the level of mere "feeling," he renounces thinking any further or specifically about what is initially called "strange" there. Yet whoever comes to terms with the strange by passing it off as what is "simply modern" stands, despite his proclaimed being "in touch with reality," within the same thoughtlessness. Or does the latter now become still greater? Indeed; for so long as something strange is taken note of in its strangeness by contrast to the habitual, the possibility persists of acknowledging something questionable within the strange. Where, on the other hand, "modernity" (keeping up with the times) is appealed to for explanation and justification, thoughtlessness has sunk into a failure to reflect, which is now elevated to the principle behind every taking of a position.

For others still, by contrast, the strange becomes ever stranger. They no longer assess the strange by pulling it back into what has gone before, and still less do they replace strangeness with an apparently unquestionable "modernity." They recognize, in what one initially feels merely to be "strange" and dissects as "modern," an indication of that worthiness that radiates out from the concealment in the essence of all things and often for a long time radiates off into emptiness. If, however, the strange becomes question-worthy, then it is never what is simply "strange" any longer, still less what is simply "modern." And in order to dwell knowingly within the question-worthiness of this strangeness, we do not even first need the public sign of World War. Those who question have an intimation of the fact that even huge and devastating slaughters will not be able to eliminate the question-worthy that is hidden within the strange.

The strangeness of this World War shows itself in multiple manifestations: the actions of battle are almost entirely still, and only from time to time does it appear as though the war were the unfurling actualization of a "plan of operation." Events of war are like interludes in the real war, which is also not identified by looking for it in the "campaigns" of press and radio, locating it in "diplomatic activity," or transforming it into an "economic war." And still, and above all: Each and every thing is drawn into this war that is seemingly not yet present at all, without one being able to properly see through how this is happening, let alone direct it.

Since the last year of the first World War, one has already experienced the encroachment of war into the entirety of human comportment and activity. Since then there has been talk of "total war." Yet the "totality" of war has here only been half comprehended, which is to say, not yet comprehended at all. "War"—for most, this is still suspended in opposition to "peace," which war perhaps fights for in being brought to an end. "World Wars" have their name initially from the process of the world, in the sense of the inhabited sphere of the earth, being overrun by them, leaving no place untouched. However, the more essential meaning of this name points to something else. The "world," in the sense of that which, as referential structure, receives into its prevailing the projective realm of historical humans, becomes warlike. War no longer fights for a state of peace, but establishes anew what the essence of peace is. Peace is now the sovereign power over all possibilities of war and the securing of the means to their accomplishment. Yet peace does not thereby become a war that is temporarily interrupted. Because the inconspicuous uncanniness of what war can be prevails still more threateningly in a state of peace, peace becomes the elimination of war. "Total" war includes peace, and such "peace" excludes "war." The distinction between war and peace becomes untenable, because both, with increasing obtrusiveness, betray themselves as equally valid, indifferent manifestations of one "totality." The "totality" of "total" war also cannot, therefore, be regarded as the belated amalgamation of the warlike and the peaceful. Rather, something else poses itself obscurely to our reflection here. What is as yet ungraspable, and yet imposing itself and intruding everywhere in the realm of the uncomprehended, is the disappearance of the distinction between war and peace. Nothing remains any longer in which the hitherto accustomed world of humankind could be salvaged; nothing of what has gone before offers itself as something that could still be erected as a goal for the accustomed self-securing of human beings.

The disappearance of the distinction between war and peace is the forcing of beings as such into the inhabitual; and its disruption of everything accustomed becomes all the more inhabitual, the more exclusively the accustomed persists and is continued. The strangeness that from time to time brushes against us provides, in the realm of the everyday, the sign of that process of the forcing of beings into the inhabitual. The strangeness is by no means an attribute of the World War that on the outside hesitates to fully break out; rather, this war itself is, in its veiled essence, already the consequence of being forced into that which withdraws from all calculative representation. The concept of the word "totality" no longer says anything; it merely designates the expansion of what has been known hitherto into what is "without remainder," and prevents an originary experiencing of that forcing of beings into the inhabitual. Yet what is this?

The disappearance of the distinction between war and peace attests to the ascendancy of power to the dominant role in the play of the world, that is, in the manner in which beings order themselves and determine their mode of rest. Power is thus the name for the being of beings. Power on each occasion seizes power over whatever it must have beneath it, so that there can be configurations and routes in which it stands and goes on the path of its essence. This path of its essence, however, is the overpowering of itself for the empowering of its unconditional status. That power seizes power over the play of the world is the ground for the ever more unrestrained eruption of the struggle for the possession of "world" power. This process can already no longer be adequately designated by employing the usual terms. If one "thinks" it and calls it "political," then one must ascribe to the "political" that "totality" that no longer says anything, and that the "economic," the "cultural," and the "technological" all lay claim to in the same manner, all in the same way failing to ascertain the essence of power. The struggle for the possession of world power becoming more acute, by contrast, makes that essence clearer. Power manifests itself—admittedly only to adequate reflection—as that which not only has no goals, but which, in the pure empowering of itself, asserts itself against every positing of a goal. This ascendancy of the essence of power as the being of all beings readily gives rise to the appearance of the "abstract." Such semblance collapses only in the moment when the supposedly "concrete"—beings that are on each occasion pursued and mastered in action—displays the character of the fleeting and almost ghostly. This moment approaches when the strange passes by from time to time, as though without a trace. The more stubbornly, however, both peaceful and belligerent struggles for world power become set on executing an unconditional empowering of power, the more pressing becomes their need, within the public realm of everyday activity, to proclaim goals and propose standpoints for common opinion. One would underestimate the inner doggedness of the will to defend "morality" in the world against alleged immorality, if one were to see in it mere hypocrisy. The process loses all semblance of merely contrived indignation only when it becomes clear that the most honest struggle to save freedom and ethical life indeed serves only to maintain and increase a possession of power whose powerfulness will not tolerate being questioned, because the preeminence of power as the being of beings has already seized power over morality and its defense as an essential means of power. And one would fall prey to a foolish underestimation of the efforts that are actively brought into play, were one not to recognize the saving of national traditions [*Volkstümer*] and the securing of one's "eternal" racial perdurance as supreme goals. Only through this does the entry into the struggle for the possession of world power receive its scope and acuity, because the positing of this goal too is a means that is set on course by power's pressing to the fore.[1] These kinds of goal-positing and the ways in which they are made public and inculcated are indispensable in the struggles for world power; for defending the "spiritual" goods of humanity and saving the "bodily" "substance" of particular humankinds must be maintained as tasks and posed anew everywhere that beings are pervasively dominated by the fundamental configuration of "metaphysics," in accordance with which spiritual "ideals" are to be realized, and their realization entails a continuous vital force of body and soul. The same configuration of metaphysics, however, is the historical ground for the essence of being as power ultimately imposing itself upon the interpretation of being as actuality and effectiveness. The positing of those goals is metaphysically necessary, not thought up and presented as fortuitous whims or "interests." Yet the positing of those same goals (the securing of "morality," the saving of "*völkisch* substance") is nevertheless always something belated that remains unknowingly and unintentionally placed into the service of the empowering of power and withdrawn from the resolute decisions of those who struggle for positions of world power. For this reason, the positing of such goals can change overnight according to the state of the struggles for the possession of power, and can even be reversed; for the point is indeed not the realization of those goals, but rather the empowering of power through the most effective *positing* of such goals in each case

---

1. Cf. Additional Materials, *Power and Race*.

and, guided by such positing, the manifold awakening and binding of effective energies and forces.

The inexorable manner in which power presses to the fore shows itself finally in the fact that the justification for the claims presented in each instance in these struggles for world power lacks credibility in the case of their defenders no less than the opponents alike. Here, the lack of credibility no longer appears at all as an ethical shortcoming in a serious or lasting manner, but rather—something that has now become much more grave—as a clumsiness pertaining to "propaganda." The ground for this complete ineffectiveness of all attempts at justification does not lie in the unsettling or indifference of the "morality of peoples." The decline of the latter, just like the ineffectiveness of the justifications, is already a consequence of the pressing to the fore of the power that in its essence rejects all goals. It bears within itself and is the self-expanding capability of being suddenly unleashed into arbitrary and yet calculated suppression and annihilation. To this end, power requires an unrestrictable capacity for transformation and the rejection of every claim to justification. Certainly, it plies itself to the semblance of the legitimacy of this demand; for the closer power comes to its ownmost essence, that is, the more it is power through its own power, the more loudly and frequently it provides for "peace and order." The latter serve only for power to subjugate the last opposition to power. With the disappearance of every opposition, the space is eliminated from out of which a claim upon power that is foreign to power could rise up against power in general. Power replaces all possibility of legitimacy with the unconditional empowering of itself. The justification of power does not even need to be rejected any longer; power has removed all "meaning" from it. For "right" is now the title for demands that are granted and "freedoms" that are needed in a distribution of power. And with this the possibility also disappears of passing off power as mere "arbitrariness." Power's pressing to the *fore* has the form of an inexorable retraction of every possibility of determining power by way of something that it itself is not. This indicates that with power, everything is concerned with the exclusive empowering of its essence, which finds itself in the unconditional overpowering of itself. This is why whatever it brings under it is of no concern to it, while by contrast the possibility of unrestricted subjugation indeed means everything. This possibility secures power for itself in a manner that cannot be resisted. From the outset it admits a being as a being only insofar as it is makeable. Makeability consists in the being's being able to be planned and calculated and, as thus represented, being able to be produced at any time. This malleability of beings furnishes the precondition for the possibility of the deployment of the human being belonging to a corresponding humankind, one for whom all reflection can now count only as a mistake. To such possibility of deployment at any time, arbitrary and withdrawn from all negotiation, there belongs the replaceability of each by each; through the malleability of beings, that is, through the empowering of power to the being of beings, the humankind in question receives the stamp of "human material" that can be dispensed arbitrarily. It is not the deployment of the human being that makes beings makeable; rather, the malleability demanded by the essence of power forces all comportment toward beings into the "readiness for deployment" that gets promoted to its most prominent distinguishing feature. The power that, with the aid of the malleability of beings has attained power over its own overpowering, thereby reveals its essence for the first time. This essence does not first lie within power as the capability for domination that disposes over the means of all forces. This still does not yet think power back into itself, but rather in the direction of its "external expression." In itself, power is the unconditioned domain of making of the overpowering of itself and of the malleability subservient to it. What essentially prevails in this domain of making is *machination:* directing oneself toward the empowering of power and the malleability of all beings to which this empowering is directed in advance, because it is demanded in advance from out of overpowering.

This malleability enjoins beings into the unlimited and constant securing of their presence; in such malleability the *configuration* of ἐνέργεια and of ἰδέα that metaphysically characterizes modernity shows itself.

Power lays claim to this malleability so essentially that it subscribes to it entirely as the sole essencing of being and goes back into the ground of its essence: the "domain of making" [*die "Mache"*].

In machination, being's falling off in the commencement into the constancy of its essential absencing attains the supreme corruption of its essence.

Conventionally, the term "machination" refers to *human* undertakings that are intent on gaining advantages and on deception under the semblance of harmless activities. "Machination" as a human "posture" first comes into play to an unrestrained degree where the humankind in question already stands in the midst of beings whose being, as power, intensifies its essence to the extreme of machination. Machination as naming the essence of *being,* however, is not the extension or transfer to beings as a whole of a merely human conduct. By contrast, the essence of power demands a particular humankind for its enforcement as the enjoined ordering of beings as a whole, as soon as being passes over into the unrestricted empowering of its power essence into machination. The petty deceitfulness of mere human "machination" is but an approximation, inaccessible to itself, to the way in which being as machination essentially escapes our grasp within the public manifestation of beings that is permitted by machination. The more "purely" machination dominates the play of being, the more exclusively beings attain priority in their malleability. The more obtrusively beings become entrenched in malleability and lend to humankind the illusion of beings being the construct of their "intervention," the more securely the machination whose power pervades everything conceals itself within such illusion. What it properly conceals is its essence, in everywhere showing the trace of its essential prevailing, a trace that is undeciphered and at most misinterpreted. Machination is the ground of the inhabitual into which all beings are forced, in such a way that it appears more and more self-evident that beings on the one hand lie present before us as something useful, and on the other are the successful result of human undertakings. Boundless disposal over beings and the most rapid promotion of their use, unhindered planning of the crushing of all resistance and the public extinguishing of every reservation concerning the succeeding of such measures indeed confirm everywhere and constantly the priority of beings over being, which has apparently vanished into nothing and with this appears to be nothing. Yet that which simply confirms the priority of beings cannot be the ground of such priority. Yet what if the ground of this priority of beings were that which announces itself as the ground of the inhabitual? What if, within the inhabitual that surrounds all beings and unexpectedly impresses itself upon us from out of every being, and nevertheless remains ungraspable, beyng were to veil itself?

The inhabitual and a humankind's being forced into it are indeed grounded in machination. Machination first unveils itself as beyng that has apparently been thrust aside into nothing, and the provenance of this illusion becomes clearer, when the inhabitual has become more essentially prevalent and every obstacle has been removed from the path of its becoming obtrusive.

The inhabitual at first manifests itself in the leveling out of the distinction between war and peace. "World War" is not at all the very struggle for the possession of world power. "World Wars" can count only as the interludes of a more essential process in which the inhabitual is grounded and out of which it first unveils itself completely. Within what process, however, is the interlude "World War" suspended? The process is pervaded by "interest" in the possession of world power. Such "interests" parade various "ideals" before them in each case, ideals whose desirability spurs on the need for power.

The need for power seeks the means of its fulfillment and finds those means in its disposing over every force and all resources. The growing disposing over force fuels the addiction to power. This addiction serves the empowering of power as the implicit authoritative "interest," and is itself first released into its unconditional essence by the empowering of power on each occasion. Even the possession of world power is not the goal of power's empowering, because this empowering knows no goal-positing. The possession of world power remains only an end attributed to the addiction to power, an end through whose fulfillment the empowering of power is accomplished, and in such a way that the possession of world power precisely never attains dominance over power, but rather is compelled to subserve it. The struggles for world power betray from time to time the process of the empowering of power in the direction of the unconditional aspect of machination, yet are not themselves this empowering. This empowering is indeed the hinge of the historicality of the entire history of the modern era that is marked as world war.

The empowering of power into its powerfulness, however, makes itself known yet at the same time hides itself within those implementations of power and institutions of power that are habitually familiar under the title of "political events and circumstances." Nevertheless, one would like to find the essence of power and thereby power's empowering directly and most assuredly within the "realm" of the "political," especially if "politics" is no longer an isolated domain of human action, but has rather assumed the all-determinative control and provision for a particular humankind amid beings. Political planning and action indeed show power relations and power struggles in a particular light. However, the essence of power in the sense of power's becoming empowered into its unconditional aspect becomes visible here only if the political itself is already experienced in terms of beings as such and the humankind that belongs to them.

Initially one looks for the "seat" of the political implementation of power and of the institution of power that directs it within the "historically" familiar forms of state and of government. One even finds that it is especially the "authoritarian" states that give free rein to the pure implementation of power. The "parliamentary" states assess this implementation of power as the blind raging of an uninhibited lust for force, as distinct from the distribution of power that they themselves procure. The play of power here transpires under the auspices of "free" negotiation, and this illusion gives rise to another one, namely, that such an implementation of power would alone be "ethical," as opposed to the "authoritarian" exercise of force. This reciprocal judging and condemning of fundamental political positions indeed also belongs to the form of their implementation of power. Yet it also prevents essential insight into the *metaphysical* sameness (determined from out of beings as such as a whole) of these modern configurations of the political implementation of power. This sameness is attested to in a dual manner. Each of the fundamental political positions asserts itself in proclaiming an "ideal": an "idea" of human community and the procurement of its happiness is posited as the standard for bringing about the peace and order of the "real," and thus of reconfiguring it. On the other hand, however, this "idea" is determined as "democracy," which grants the authoritative position of power to the "people." Any doubt concerning the identity in metaphysical essence of these forms of state completely shatters in view of the fact that, each in a different manner and in the kind of publicness shaped by each, they both propagate the same public illusion that power would be apportioned to "the people." This illusion belongs to the way in which the institution of power operates within a particular political implementation of power. Yet the perpetrating of this illusion is not a charge of deception that can be made against the possessors of political power, just as the people's opinion that power could ever be "with the people" cannot be regarded as mere stupidity. The "democratic" illusion is awakened and maintained just as much by the governed as by those who "govern"; for this illusion that power would "belong" to all and would be distributed to all—whereas in truth it belongs to no one—springs from the essence of power, for whose empowering all possessors of power remain only those who are unknowingly overpowered as such, those in whose conduct power makes known and hides its powerfulness in a peculiar manner. This veiling of the proper possession of power within the empowering of power is therefore to be encountered especially where the implementation of power no longer has a merely political character, but a directly metaphysical one, in despotism and dictatorship. Here all power seems to be exclusively "in the hands" of a single individual who satisfies his "subjective" lust for power by oppressing the never-too-many. One fails to consider the fact that such individuals, as possessors of power, not only stand under the opposing power of the oppressed, an opposing power that indeed does not belong to the oppressed either; the "despot" also stands under the power of the completeness of his own power. Indeed, "despots" and "dictators" can least of all *be* the possessors of power they appear to be, provided that they are genuine dictators, and that is to say, executors of the empowering of power to overpowering into the unconditional nature of its essence. For empowering demands two things. On the one hand, the gathering of the disposal of all power into a unity that powerfully maintains this disposal in its possible intensification, a gathering that prevents in advance every exception. That is to say: the possession of power must unfold the possibility of overpowering ever anew from out of itself. This possibility, however, undermines dictatorship, because the latter brings with it a petrification at one level of power and excludes itself from the open realm of the unconditional. On the other hand, the empowering of power demands the assimilation of all forms of power, and of all those who have thereby been placed under power, into *uniform*ity. This uniformity also removes every mark of distinction from that possession of power that is alone appropriate to the essence of the unconditional empowering of power, and does so in such an essential manner that it ruthlessly thrusts the possessors of power into inconspicuousness.

The uniformity that essentially prevails in power's empowering is not an empty homogeneity of power relationships, but rather the fundamental law, unfolded in terms of power itself, of that impulse which impels power into the unconditional nature of its essence. On occasion the implementation of power betrays this fundamental law of all empowering of power in a scarcely heeded and still less pondered phenomenon: the more power finds its way into its essence, that is, intensifies itself, the more forceful the impulse toward the intensification of power becomes. The more forcefully this impulse imposes itself, however, the more decisively it asserts itself as what is "natural." Power's empowering thus betrays its "nature," that is, the ground of the conditions of its possibility: unconditional empowering of itself into limitless power over itself that requires no goal. The continual intensification of power is not some lack of restraint that it first exploits, but rather the integrity of its ownmost "nature," in accordance with which the assimilation of everything and everyone into the common element (*commune*) of unconditional empowering regulates the impulse of power in advance. Power's empowering into the unconditional aspect of machination and from out of the latter is the essence of *"communism."* What goes by this name is here thought neither "politically" nor "sociologically," neither in terms of "worldview" nor "anthropologically," indeed not even merely "metaphysically," but is conceived rather as that ordering of beings as such and as a whole that marks the historical era as that of the consummation, and thereby of the end, of all metaphysics. This concept of "communism," thought from out of the history of beyng, may at first seem very arbitrary, especially as it does not directly name those "communistic" phenomena that are historiographically familiar. For the conventional term "communism" means the common pertaining to the equal: that each within this "order" of a particular humankind has to work equally much, to earn equally much, to consume equally much,

## Κοινόν. Out of the History of Beyng [191–193]

and to have an equal degree of pleasure, where these accomplishments and needs at the same time exhaust the acknowledged whole of human "life," in that they map out what in general should be taken to be "real" and what is to count as "the world." Here, making everything be in common forces each into the uniform averageness of all. The "political" sign of this force appears as the revolution of bourgeois class society into the classless state. To those hitherto excluded from the possession and enjoyment of all goods in existing society, the guiding motif of the "proletarian" "uprising" imposes itself: the nationalization of industry and banks, the distribution of large-scale land holding, the abolition of monasteries, and the elimination of the "intelligentsia" in favor of the "specialization" that is indeed needed for the labor process. In this way, the many that were previously oppressed and are henceforth the never-too-many see themselves rise from the elimination of class distinctions to become the sole authoritative class. The opportunity granted them to exploit those who previously exploited them gives rise to that representation of the "real" and to that assessment of "life" that count as the "political worldview" of "communism." In accordance with this view, it seems as though a mass of human beings called the "proletariat," who previously floundered in oppression, are now liberated, stripped of their essence as "mere" masses, installed as the one and only "party," and thereby brought to power. In truth, however, instituting this one and only "party" first creates the essence of the masses, in that it shapes in advance the uniformity of comportment and the uniform sameness of attitude in conducting and assessing all things. Only within the unequivocal contours of this stamping can the mass human being appear as such. "Communism," therefore, does not gather together the "proletariat of all lands" who are supposedly already at hand in themselves, but rather first of all transposes a humankind into the "proletariat," by forcing it into the accomplishment of that uniformity pertaining to making things be in common, which appears as the seizing of power on the part of the "people." The proletariat is "liberated," however, only so as to bring its essence into play, that is, to be of service to a power that it can neither understand nor is permitted to know at all. For this power itself constantly forces the proletariat out of any need to inquire concerning a power "beyond" it, because it—power—gives the proletariat the illusion that it—the proletariat—is in sole possession of all power. Due to its provenance from a revolution that must always remain a *counter-movement*, power appears to the "proletariat" in the guise of bourgeois forms of "influence" and "worth." In the realm over which the proletariat disposes, as the sole bearer of a single "worldview," there now lie all the things desired by the bourgeoisie that has been eliminated: "class consciousness," "party rule," regulating the "standard of living," promoting "progress," and the creation of "culture." The proletariat indeed possesses all of this. How should it not be of the opinion that it possesses power as well? Yet the driving power in communism is that which seduces everyone into the enchantment of the uniformity and homogeneity of all. In the face of this power, which constitutes the essential ground of the proletariat, the proletariat is impotent, so definitively so that such power makes use of this impotence in order to secure and intensify the empowering of its essence.

The accomplishment of this power, the empowering of whose essence is "communism," is neither confined to being exercised by an authority of state government nor does it exhaust itself in the play of forces belonging to the power of a political party, but rather in its fundamental intent its power permeates in advance beings as a whole and the particular humankind included therein. The possession of power is thus in general withheld from the human being, and yet there must be power-possessors who direct the play of power within a "space" in which every claim to power is prevented in advance, and there is not, for instance, merely the elimination of the factual validity of individuals and groups. Such possessors of power can only be a few; for it is only the just-a-few who guarantee a uniform implementation of all available means of power that can be directed from a center and gathered back into this center. It is the just-a-few alone who are also capable of securing the possibilities of new and unanticipated forms of power and of directing their surprising actualization. Only such a few ensure that in the disposal of power the ruthlessness of its deployment is relentless and yet the inconspicuousness of measures taken is maintained. Power-possession, thus configured, in itself pursues a constant increase in power.

The "just-a-few" in no way refers only to a small number of deployers of force as distinct from the innumerable "powerless" masses, but rather designates the characteristic nature of a particular possession of power. The possessors of power that accord with this do not "have" power as their own so as to wreak some personal capriciousness with it, and for this reason they also *are* not who they are as prominent individuals. Every public naming and appreciation of their actions carries within it the danger of mis-directing and weakening the deployment of power by such orientation toward the public. This is why power demands of its possessors that they remain nameless and their operations inaccessible. And thus they use and exploit all the more frequently a public supply of those in whose conduct the masses recognize their own "will." The empowering of power (i.e., communism) creates for itself the most incisive securing of its pure deployment in the kind of agreement by virtue of which the just-a-few are *united* in their possession of power. Their being with one another consists neither in some "sentimental" "camaraderie," nor in being blindly sworn to conspiracy, but rather in that cold distrust from which each watches over the other and in this way binds himself to the other. Such distrust is never nourished by the petty fear of a reduction in one's personal possession of power. It stems from a profound anxiety in the face of any inappropriate disturbance in the empowering of power that could have as its consequence a petrification of power at a level that has already been attained. Such essential anxiety, which, in order truly to be able to be an anxiety, must beforehand already have put behind it any unease concerning the personal fate of the possessors of power, is the fundamental attunement of the just-a-few. Genuine anxiety, which in its many shapes only ever springs from an exposure to beings as such as a whole in each case, can pervasively attune one's stance and comportment only where the latter are thoroughly governed by a daring courage that in turn is not merely summoned up by the strength of personal will but is bequeathed as dowry from out of a directedness into beings as a whole and through the latter. Thus there arises too the non-public namelessness of the just-a-few, a namelessness by virtue of which they are as though they simply were not, belonging to the same directedness into the deployment of power's empowering, a directedness already removed from every choice. Namelessness, however, extends to all essential operations and states of affairs in "communistic" reality. It is thus the reflection of that assimilation of all power relationships into homogeneity. Uniformity alone gives the power of unconditional empowering power over itself. Power "belongs" neither to the "people," nor to an individual, nor even to those just-a-few. Power tolerates no possessors. This unconditional intolerance prevailing in the essence of power's empowering is characteristic of communism. Yet power does not rule for the sake of power, which is to say: for the mere exercise of a force that has just been attained; that always means a relapse into the petrification of a power that in truth remains impotent against the essence of power. Power rules for the sake of empowering itself into its essence, that is, machination. "Communism" is power's permeating beings as such with the empowering of power into machination as power's unconditionally instituting itself upon the previously erected malleability of all beings. "Communism" would be thought in too harmless a manner, were one to abhor it or celebrate it as the monstrous outgrowth of some human addiction, whether to "revenge," or to "happiness," or to mere violence. "Communism" is not at all something "human." "Subhumankind" may be the slave, the "overman" may be the sovereign master of communism who only apparently has power over himself, yet everywhere the human being is admitted merely as the executor, ossified within what has been his essence hitherto (*animal rationale*), of that permeating of beings by power by virtue of their malleability. Ever since machination, as the essence of being, has begun to assume the power of sovereignty over beings, "communism" must, initially for the most part in unrecognized disguises, yet relentlessly—because it cannot be stopped by individual beings, and not at all by beings—become the constitution of being pertaining to the world epoch of modernity that is beginning its consummation.

In the empowering of power into machination as its essence, the impetus of power that has been unleashed into the unconditional overflows all resistances, for only what already stands under the dominion of machination is admitted as "real." Since, however, the empowering of the essence of power becomes historical in "communism," *it* is what drives the expansion and consolidation of the impetus of power into the intolerance that is bereft of every condition. Thoroughly refusing every possession of power on the part of every human effort and presumption, "communism" turns neither to the destinies of the peoples who struggle to assert themselves in the aftermath of the course hitherto taken by history, nor does it heed the strivings, wishes, or convictions of human groups within the peoples, among whom individuals still remain scattered in apparent isolation. Yet even this manner in which the humankind of modernity is swept away into the orbit of machination is only the first, superficial manifestation of the intolerance pertaining to communism, and not yet its essential fury. The reach of the latter will be such that all customary relations to the beings hitherto familiar will be ruptured, in that beings will nowhere offer any longer the support or shelter that they previously granted. Everyday affairs indeed take their course; one indeed becomes accustomed even to the "strange" and to war. Yet amid the appearances cast by an inconspicuousness that is not even heeded, this becoming accustomed confirms the unsettling of beings and of all relations to them under the power of the inhabitual that has apparently been parried. The unsettling unleashed within the intolerance that pertains to "communism" points to a destruction whose empowering belongs to the essence of machination.

With this destruction, whose corrupt essence in machination manifests itself only at certain moments, the inhabitual begins to prepare itself for a transformation of the essence of history for which the replacement of the previous world epoch by a "newest" one can only ever be an ambiguous sign.

The at first merely "strange" aspect of contemporary conditions and states of affairs becomes ever more strange in that now even characterizing beings and our active residence amidst them as "strange" or "unusual" becomes noticeably more suspect. The harbingers of a history that will be other in essence demand a knowledge of machination that will not evade it by any cover-up, and will thus stand within its uncircumventable domination, yet will nonetheless withstand it. Yet this withstanding cannot lie in somehow fending off the powering of machination, and nor, therefore, can it mean the salvaging and reestablishment of what has been up to now. Withstanding here is not the preservation of what is in essence already past, albeit still "modern," but is rather a withstanding in transition to erecting a site for what is to come. The withstanding of machination is a standing within the transition that is already in process with the unconditional empowering of machination. The steadfast insistence of this standing within occurs in the manner of a knowing that is more active than all deeds done in the service of machination, because in keeping with its essence it needs no success, but rather is what it is, in that it *is*.

Truly *being* in the midst of beings that prevail in essence by way of machination means to know machination in a transitional manner as an event of beyng, and to belong to the question-worthiness of the truth of beyng. Truly being in the midst of beings pervaded by the power of machination cannot, therefore, signify simply becoming habituated to the strange and inhabitual, so as then to swallow something inevitable in some kind of "heroism"; all heroism belongs to the already passing "world" of machination and is insufficient for a steadfast insistence within the transition.

Taking a stand on the grounds of this steadfast insistence is knowing. Its essence remains closed off and its essential accomplishment impossible so long as "knowing" is practiced in the sense of representation and cognition as determined by machination. It is irrelevant whether one here employs such cognition simply as a means to action, or even permits it as "theoretical" deliberation and bestows upon it the distinction of "constructive thinking"; for the latter is certainly the purest form of that "communistic" reckoning that is subservient solely to the empowering of machination.

Draft for Κοινόν
On the History of Beyng

## The End of Modernity in the History of Beyng

The metaphysical token of the consummation of modernity is the historical empowering of the essence of "communism" into the constitution of being belonging to the epoch of consummate meaninglessness. The meaning-less is here understood in terms of the concept of meaning thought in *Being and Time*. In accordance with this concept, meaning is the realm of projection for the projecting of being upon its truth; and truth means the unconcealing release of being into the clearedness of its essencing, clearing of self-concealing. Refusal prevails essentially within it. Which, clearing itself, is the beckoning of beyng. Beckoning, beyng gathers itself into the bestowal of itself as singular. No correlation to beings is capable of bringing it to language.

The "meaning-less" means the truth-less: the *remaining absent of the clearing* of being. Meaninglessness comes to be consummated by this absence remaining in unrecognizability and together with this, being disappearing into forgotten oblivion. "Being" counts only as the unquestioned, most general word for what is most universal and empty; beings have unconsidered priority. That which is makes itself known and asserts itself in the claim to be thoroughly makeable, and consequently plannable and calculable. Offering themselves in this way, beings compel in human beings the exclusive prerogative of the domain of making. The unrelenting aspect of their boundless coursings casts a spell upon humankind that leads them only ever to regard those beings that can be made as everything. "Being"—being's abandonment—consummation of meaning-lessness.

When meaninglessness becomes consummated, "values" (values of life and culture) are proclaimed as the supreme goals and kinds of goal for human beings. "Values" are only ever the surreptitious translation of truthless being into mere slogans for what counts as valuable and accountable within the singular sphere of makeability. And the valuing pertaining to the revaluation of all values, in whatever direction it may be accomplished, is the ultimate banishment into consummate meaninglessness. The emergence of the manifold forms in which value is thought confirms that beings have been delivered over fully to being's abandonment. To the powerless values there corresponds the impotence of representations of value. Such impotence favors the erupting of the *power* of beings that prevail in essence from out of makeability.

Beingness has dissolved into pure machination, in such a way that through this machination, beings attain unlimited power and being's abandonment of beings assumes its concealed "rule." The latter does not stem from that power of machination but springs from the concealed history of beyng. Machination alone can place itself exclusively under an empowering toward itself and find in this something ultimate. Where meaninglessness attains power, and does so through the human being as *subjectum*, the one who calculates and marshals the calculability of himself and of all things, there the elimination of all meaning (i.e., of the question concerning the truth of beyng and/or its resonance within beingness and its projecting) must be replaced by what alone remains admissible as an appropriate replacement: by a *reckoning*, and indeed by reckoning with "values." "Value" is the translation of the truth of essence into amount and the gigantic; the supreme power of the "thought of value" confirms that beings have been fully delivered over to accountability.

Conceived in a thoughtful manner, *"communism"* does not consist in the fact that each has to work equally much, earn an equal amount, consume an equal amount, and have equal pleasure, but rather in the fact that all modes of comportment and attitudes adopted by all are compelled in the same way by the unconditional power of an unnamed few. Decisionlessness (the breaking off of every possible growth of a decision and of every assuming of one) becomes the average air breathed by all. This common aspect, making each common to all, is as though it did not happen; that industry is nationalized, likewise the banks, that large-scale land holdings are dissolved, monasteries abolished, that every knowing is falsified into "intelligence" and the latter alone finds a "specialist" use and thereby "reality" within the domain of specialists;[a] that the manufacturing of a "public opinion" of the so-called "people" by press and radio is only out to maintain a fictitious construct that fundamentally no one takes seriously apart from those who have power, and that the latter too regard only as one means of power among others—all of this, from the perspective of the possessions and demeanor of the bourgeoisie hitherto, may appear as a real loss and destruction. However, this nationalization of "society" into the state signifies little, insofar as the state has become only a subordinate tool of the one and only party; the party itself, however, the tool of the Soviets, and the Soviets the forum of the few. It is characteristic of them that they remain unnamed, and the oft-named (Stalin and his publically active entourage) are in each instance tolerated only as the front men.

The "just-a-few" by no means refers to a small number by contrast with the countless many who are excluded from the possession of power. The "just-a-few" pursue their own manner of gathering every empowering of power into the sheer ruthlessness of unconditional

---

a. Trs.: Reinterpretation, elimination.

procedure. Only the few guarantee the unbounded and secure character of the most inconspicuous implementation of power. This way of proceeding is metaphysically determined, spurred on and stirred up solely by being's abandonment, unrecognizable as such, of all beings. Only through such a few[b] can the agreement be secured in an unconditional and uncompromised way, that "welfare," partaking in the advances made by culture, the elimination of distinctions of class and profession, and treating governed and "governors" as equal are merely pretexts for the "people," before which the "people" stand entranced and thus cannot at all strive to see beyond them into that which alone is: the power of the few. Once more: It is not that these few are the possessors of power, but rather that their "resoluteness" alone everywhere maintains the unimpeachable priority of the complete power of institutions over against every attempt at independent insight or assertion of the will on the part of individuals or groups.[c]

The despotism of the few does not, therefore, have its grounds in the personal lust for power on the part of individual "subjects"; rather, the latter are for their part, and without their knowing it, merely exploited as the bearers and "place holders" of the unconditional empowering of pure power with the single goal of letting power install itself in its own institutions and securing for it the status of what is truly real. Whoever speaks of *"materialism"* here attests only to how much representation is still left clinging to the scraps that one or other school of thought has thrown out there for the "people." This "materialism" is *"spiritual"* in the highest sense, so decisively that the consummation of the essence of spirit belonging to Western metaphysics must be recognized in it.[d] Lenin knew this clearly. And this is why the "danger" of communism does not consist in its economic and social consequences; it consists, rather, in the fact that its *spiritual* essence, its essence as spirit, is not recognized, and the debate is placed on a level that entirely ensures the supreme power of communism and the inability to resist it.[e] The historical power of communism and its proper essence[f] as oligarchic Soviet power is the simplest and most compelling counter-proof against the allegedly Nietzschean doctrines, propa-

---

b. Trs.: The few and the non-public most sheerly related to publicness. How! Why this. The non-public as form of power. In its form inconspicuously thrust [?] upon the habitual—the grand slogans—the invention of names.

c. Trs.: Concerning Russia—few know—even if more familiar, no longer to be *known!*

d. Trs.: *Essence.*

e. Trs.: This sounds as though it could still be stopped and turned back.

f. Trs.: Its *spiritual* essence stymies decisions.

gated by those who exploit Nietzsche, concerning the "impotence" of "spirit." This is why the "struggle"[g] by the Christian churches against Bolshevism, for instance, is unable to achieve anything, because they are not able to recognize its spiritual essence, since they themselves are subservient to something "spiritual" that essentially and definitively prevents Christendom from ever founding in opposition to this "world enemy Bolshevism" a site of decisive questioning that would be entirely different in essence and uproot it from the ground up. It is above all only ever through "struggle" that degenerates into sham fights and eventual agreement that the knowledge must awaken that that pure power in its unconditional empowering for its part points back to something else as its origin and essential support. That is *"machination"*; and this word is meant to think an essential decision in the Western history of beyng. Such *thinking* comes infinitely closer to the "reality" of the occurrences of the epoch (and not as actionless gaping) than every kind of petty bourgeois "intervention." It would admittedly be an erroneous demand ever to want to see this thinking transformed into a universal form of representing and opining practiced by everyone. By contrast, one thing is needed: a knowing of the many uncircumventable and essentially diverse forms in which the historical overcoming of communism must transpire. The most stubborn impediment to this knowing remains the unnamed and poorly considered expectation of an eventual return of pre-communistic, bourgeois conditions. This beguiling expectation continually feeds on the erroneous perspective for which whatever is "public" alone appears to be what is real, whereas it is, after all, only the indeed necessary and never simply to be leapt over, yet empty shadow of history, which essences only as the history of beyng.

It is not flight before the essential content of political reality and into the "spiritual," but rather thinking through the political into the ground of the boundless essence of its power that attains those realms from which "spirit," as a dominant form of metaphysics, may be overcome together with metaphysics itself. And only where "spirit" is active in advance as a model or counter-model does the opinion that the spiritual is rooted in the "bodily" achieve its respect, its understandability, and the possible validity of a profession of faith as a worldview. "Communism," however, is no mere form of state, nor simply a kind of political worldview, but rather the *metaphysical* constitution in which the humankind of modernity finds itself as soon as the consumma-

---

g. Trs.: "Struggle": 1. On a plane least one's own [?]. 2. In general not what is decisive—what is the point of struggle, where "justification" as *power* is of such a kind that it makes such things superfluous.

tion of modernity begins its final stage. Accustomed to spending this "life" within a sphere of recognized operations (of welfare—and the promotion of culture) and covered by the protective roof of believed salvations ("eternal bliss"), the human being today—since those securities are slowly coming to appear as having long since become fragile and groundless—is entering that cluelessness that vacillates in all directions and that now allows him only to be on the lookout for "goals" that are supposed to exceed what has gone before and that must thereby precisely rush headlong into what is the same *in kind*. For if beyond the cultivation of competence and the pleasurable aspect of bodily life there remains nothing more than the unconditional expansion of this "goal" to the entire mass of humans who find pleasure and health, are industrialized and technicized and make culture, in a process that continually registers the intensification of these life interests anew; and if even the will of the peoples of Europe is *not* capable of avoiding war, either for the purpose of asserting those "interests" that have long since become their possession, or indeed in order to assure the attainment of the satisfaction of these "interests," then the mass war that is forcibly brought about as necessarily pressing within the essence of those interests and that is correspondingly instituted to an unconditional degree confirms the fact that the modern human being still stands everywhere within that which has gone before, that is, within beings as determined metaphysically.

The helpless entanglement in beings is unable to experience what is nearest, namely, that here, flight in the face of beyng determines history in its essence. This gives rise to a situation that, along with a complete securing of one's entire life and of its spheres of interest, indeed lets the uncertainty of a decision assume the dimensions of the ungraspable. The threat to being human from out of that which constitutes precisely the unconditional mastery of a secure directing of all measures of consolidation, the threat that is intangibly intimated and at the same time rejected once more as an illusion, gives advance notice of something that the modern human being, who administers and defrays metaphysics to the end, is never able to experience. It cannot be experienced by him, not because it lies at some remote distance over beyond his habitual domains, but because it is so *near* to him that the human being bent on making secure must constantly have already leapt over what thus lies nearest to his concealed essence. What lies nearest is not, however, near to the "body," and not near to the "soul," and not near to the "spirit" of the human being, but is unrelated to all that; presumably, it is near[h] to the concealed ground of the essence of

---

h. Trs.: Near because *nearness itself: Da*-sein.

the human: to steadfast insistence within the truth of beyng, by virtue of which the human being can be befallen by insecurity amid his securely instituted pursuit of the secure, and can be tossed back and forth within the alternating and receding of goals, and can thereby experience what is utterly nihilative (the beckoning of the nothing). The nothing, however, is not "nothing"[i] but rather only the simplest shape of the essence of beyng, the one that is most difficult to withstand. Only on rare occasions of its concealed history does beyng convey the middle of the essence of the human and properly assign it to the relation to beyng, a relation that is not a representing, and not at all any kind of "lived experiencing," but instead the grounding of the truth of beyng, a grounding that at times has yet to happen. This essential middle of the human never subsists independently anywhere, but first *"comes to be"* in the event of the human being's being appropriated into Dasein, and is only from out of this event. The human being cannot "make" this history and can never intervene in it; as himself the one seized by its essence, he is capable only of preparing the time when he will be struck (conveyed into the middle) by what is most to come in that which is coming from the remoteness of what is nearest. So long as the human being remains outside of this preparation, he staggers back and forth between blocked exits at the end of a long dead-end street. He has forgotten to take the path back, not back into what has gone before, indeed, but back into the commencement, whose supremacy was at once avoided by Western humankind. In what it retains, the commencement beckons the most distant future toward it. Guarding its essence gives thinking the preponderance of its questioning with a view to what is most to come. The commencement is the secret of history; for the commencement brings itself into the sudden clearing of the suddenness of beyng toward the nothing, a bringing itself that belongs to the essencing of beyng itself.

If "communism" is the metaphysical constitution of peoples in the last stage of the consummation of modernity, then this entails that already at the beginning of modernity it must set its essence into power, albeit in an as yet hidden manner. Politically, this occurs in the history of the modern English state. The latter—thought with respect to its essence while disregarding its contemporary forms of government, society, and faith—is *the same* as the state of the united Soviet republics, only with the difference that there an immense deception in the semblance of morality and the education of peoples makes all implementation of power harmless and self-evident, whereas here, modern "consciousness" exposes itself more ruthlessly in the essence

---

i. Trs.: *"Nihilism"* still metaphysics.

of its own power, although not without an appeal to bringing happiness to the people. The bourgeois Christian form of English "Bolshevism" is the most dangerous. Without its annihilation, modernity continues to be maintained.^j

The definitive annihilation, however, can only take the form of an essential self-annihilation, which is promoted most forcefully by one's own illusory essence becoming inflated into the role of savior of morality. The historiographical point in time at which the self-annihilation of "communism" sets in with a visible process and end is a matter of indifference compared to the decision that has already taken place in terms of the history of beyng and that makes that self-annihilation inevitable. The self-annihilation has its initial form in the fact that "communism" presses on in the direction of the outbreak of war-like entanglements that tend toward the unrelenting unleashings of its entire power. War is not, as Clausewitz still thinks, the continuation of politics by other means; if "war" means "total war," that is, war that springs from the *unleashed machination* of beings, then it becomes a *transformation* of "politics" and *revealer* of the fact that "politics" and every pursuit of life by means of planning have themselves only been a way of accomplishing unmastered metaphysical decisions in a manner that no longer has power over itself. Such war does not perpetuate something already at hand, but rather forces what is at hand into executing essential decisions that it itself does not master. For this reason, such war no longer admits "victors and vanquished";^k all become slaves of the history of beyng, for which they were found to be too small from the commencement and therefore compelled into war. "Total war" forces "politics," the more "real" it already is, all the more inevitably into the form of a mere execution of the demands and urgencies of beings abandoned by being, beings that can secure for themselves in a calculative manner the supreme power of the constant overpowering of the pure implementation of power, and do so solely by honing and instituting unconditional plannability. That such war no longer knows "victors and vanquished" lies not in the fact that both are enlisted to an equal degree and in one way or another suffer equally great damages but rather is grounded in the fact that the opponents *both and on every occasion* must remain within what is essentially undecided. The unmistakable sign of this is that they know and take account of nothing other than their "interests." War itself *does not permit* one or other of them to let these "interests" become worthy of question in general or indeed as such with regard to their possible

---

j. Trs.: I.e., its consummation is delayed.
k. Trs.: More pointedly.

character as "goals." The promoting of world wars as a conscious tactic in the unfolding of metaphysical communism into the fundamental constitution of beings was recognized, encouraged, and practiced for the first time by Lenin. His jubilation over the outbreak of world war in the year 1914 knows no limits. The more modern such world wars become, the more ruthlessly they demand the consolidation of all forces pertaining to war within the power possessed by a few. This means, however, that nothing whatsoever that in any way belongs to the being of peoples could be exempted from being an element of force for war. And precisely this instituting of beings with a view to the unlimited solidifying of the unfolding of power into the measurelessness of the mostly inconspicuous and immediately self-evident incorporation of everything, which was recognized for the first time by Lenin as "total mobilization" and indeed named as such, is actualized by world wars. It carries "communism" to the highest level of its essence in machination. This supreme "height" is the only site suitable for the downward plunge into the nothing of being's abandonment that it has already prepared, and for initiating the long end of its coming to an end.

All peoples of the Western world are drawn into this process, in each case in accordance with the historical determination of their essence. They must accelerate it or inhibit it. They may labor to veil it or to expose it. They can seemingly combat it or attempt to remain outside of its limitless field of operation.

In the meantime, however, another history of beyng has already commenced; for when beings as a whole (here and now, those of machination) drive toward the end, there must be another commencement of beyng. The concealed shape of this commencement is indeed such that only those rare and futural ones can think and poetize it in an unfamiliar knowing. Such commencing of a commencement is, however, its most worthy and richest legacy of its own essence to the history of the grounding of its truth in those beings that are arising. What is the significance of the appearing of the enormous frenzy of devastation that accompanies machination and of the "deeds" triggered by it, compared to the coming of the last god and the silent dignity of expectation assigned him? Yet the god—how so, the god? Ask beyng! And in its silence, in the inceptual essence of the word, the god answers. You may wander through each and every being. Nowhere does the trace of the god show itself. You can rearrange all beings, never will you encounter a free place for housing the god. You may go beyond your beings and will find only the beingness once more of that which already counted as beings for you. You clarify using only that which must already count as clear for you. But ask beyng!

Yet how are you to become a questioner who asks beyng rather than investigating a being? Only through the voice of silence that tunes your essence to steadfast insistence within Da-sein and raises what has been attuned into a hearkening to the coming. For the coming alone is capable of fulfilling the essence of godship in an inceptual manner. In coming, the gods fathom the ground of the most profound history and are the harbingers of the last god, whose last is his coming. He brings nothing, unless himself; yet even then only as the most coming of that which comes. Ahead of himself, he bears the to-come of the future [*Zu-kunft*], his time-play-space in beyng, a time-play-space that itself waits for the god, in coming, to fulfill it and in coming to come. Thus is the god, of his necessity choosing beyng, the most extreme god, who knows no making or providence. The last god apportions no consolations. Inconsolability grows together with the addiction to finding in some consolation the fulfillment and plenitude of "life," an addiction fed by the opinion that "life," whether meant as "on this side" or "beyond," would be the single and highest form of being that the human being could come to have. Counting on the salvation of the soul propels one into that Dasein-less "living experience" from which the last god remains so remote that he does not even first turn away from the domains and constructs of such "life."

Beyng that is asked about, from which the last god answers in his time, attunes, however, into confidence in the bestowal of the most silent relation to the earth of a world, which, contesting their essence, open out into the site of a history of the countering of human beings and the last god. This confidence is not chained to what is at hand, nor built upon any being. It is appropriated from beyng as the ever inceptual serenity, never collapsing into habituation, of an extended courage to watch over the preparing for the event. This serenity is strong enough to take up into the essence of its confidence even terror in the face of being's abandonment of beings. In its courageous forbearance it establishes a magnanimity toward the invisible devastation of the essence of beyng, a devastation that has already exceeded all rampant destruction of beings. Perhaps, however, the human being will not have become ready for the pain of this magnanimous forbearance of the confidence in beyng for long periods to come. That confidence, however, preserves within itself the essence of joy. Metaphysics, together with all its subservient forms of ecclesiastical faith and of worldviews, lost in beings, only ever attain "pleasure" in and through beings, at most "spiritual" pleasure "of the soul." Joy is not pleasure. Joy has its origin in the commencement of the history of beyng. It shifts the end of metaphysics and thereby of modernity into what has been passed over in transition. Counter-attuned magnanimity and forbearance of the confidence in beyng say in a more expansive manner what was meant to be named in the word "care." Habitual "lived experiencing" and opining henceforth hear in this word only an indication of gloom and doom; this attests to how exclusively they think in terms of the opposite, which they know as "pleasure." And thus there arises the inability to know the essence of "care," by becoming fixated upon the metaphysics that has itself already become commonplace and its ultimate triumph: "communism" as that which humanly drives machination, driven by metaphysics itself. The "rule" of machination is the end of the first commencement of the history of beyng. The sudden breaking off in relation to this end is the other commencement of this history. In the first commencement, beyng prevails in essence as arising (φύσις); in the other commencement, beyng prevails in essence as event. Arising, machination, event *are* the history of beyng, as they free the *essence* of history from its concealment in the first commencement, through its becoming perverted into historiography, into that to which those to come think in anticipation as the grounding of the clearing of the sustainment and think in the direction of the truth of beyng.

The history of beyng casts the dice and on occasion allows the illusion that the domain of human making determines how they then fall. They fall, however, in each case in accordance with that descent through which beyng appropriates itself unto beings. This descent is known only to those who ascend. Their ascending is an entering into a readiness to watch over the nearness of beyng, from whose abyss beings are the fallout, so as to first return as the owned that has been appropriated. Beyng as event decides not only concerning the time when it clears itself into this prevailing of its essence. Beyng as event also carries within its abyss and as this abyss a transformed essence of the originarily unitary time-play-space within which history receives its future.

Until the future human being of the Western world finds his way into the simple decisions and learns to honor and to know the abyssal remoteness of the near, long reflections are necessary to unravel the tenacious confusion and to awaken the courage for reflection as the joy of Da-sein. Those "truths" that are cooked up overnight and understood [?] by everyone will then simply be ignored as empty noise. They require no refutation. Such refutation would itself only become noise and something contrived. Truth, however, prevails in essence in the silence of beyng. This silence is the nearness of the last god.

# Appendix

# Additional Materials for *The History of Beyng (1938–40)*

### For V. Tò Κοινόν

*Amor fati*—To stand before *beings*—taking them over—because they are and as they are.

αἰδώς—the awe of being directed into the opening appropriation *of beyng*.

*Beyng*—not attunement—rather beyng that which attunes, *surpassing the nothing*.

\*

*Why beyng?*
The owned—*poverty*—beyng.
Being transported into the temporal course of the history of beyng—this *rapturous transport* in itself the first transformation of essence in the direction of Da-sein.

### Machination

The violent and crude, the deceitful and unreliable belong to the essence of malice. Yet "evil," even when not regarded "morally" and used as debasement, in order to evoke abhorrence, as a metaphysical characterization fits only the *appearance* of machination, which the self-consciousness belonging to machination can still encounter without knowing its essence in a comprehensively conceptual manner. To experience the malice that pertains to machination means: to content oneself still within the sphere of its allegedly non-dangerous character and to avoid the unadorned frightfulness of its essence.

\*

1. Why are beings as such beings as a whole?
2. How does this "as a whole" become "totality" in the case of beingness as machination?
3. To what extent is "totalization" only a supplement that no longer contains any decisive interpretation of beingness?

*For VI. The Sustainment. The Essence of Power. The Necessary*

*The Essence of Power*

To what extent there belongs to power the constant bringing about of something always new. (Achievements, conquest, success, experience lived through.)

*Not being able to stop* at something *attained,* because this would undermine *overpowering.*

The "new"—as that which is to be brought about.

The *new,* however, also as that which each time veils the essence of power—namely, its *goal-lessness.*

The latter is best camouflaged through instances of *progress,* which repeatedly charm and keep a hold on and benumb *curiosity.*

\*

Powering power not something in general, but such as in the history of being. Being as machination. Absolute unleashed *subjectivity as objectivity.* To be elaborated more precisely!

\*

*The vastness of power (its endlessness) first corresponds to the nullity of its essence in the commencement.*

*For VII. The Essence of History. "Commencement." "Beyng"*

History—what it includes in its essence as grounding in sustaining and downgoing of the truth of beyng.–

Thinking—Poetizing—Questioning—Hearing.

*Preserving—appropriating over.*

All this already appropriating over, capable of sustaining, into the owned.

Yet the latter? For the sake of beyng—and this?

*Historically*—what belongs to the *essence* of *history* and *necessarily (co-) accomplishes* that essence.

*Not* in the first instance what *has "history."*

History and history.

Not squabble and pursuit of living space for "interests" of a question-worthy "life" wanting to live itself out.

Rather *struggle for a passing* of the god as igniting all the most simple human abilities.

*Capacity for the god in the essencing of the human* as ground of *historicality*. Da-*sein* "*is*" history, "is" the *opening of appropriation*.

\*

End—(no mere cessation) there, where an already inceptive commencement remains inaccessible and what arises instead is a being exiled into the vain presumptuousness of something "new" that can become only the colossal décor of what is most habitual and commonplace.

The complete end—where there is even no commencement left—there, where the downgoing is withheld and all that pertains to decision in relation to the truth of being has become impossible.

\*

History—singularity of essence in its supreme, the poverty of the simple.

Not the coherence of what is bygone and its historiographical retention.

The wealth of the multiple.

Da-sein—resonance of the voice of the event as steadfast insistence of silence.

Through the overcoming of metaphysics, the *historiographical* perspective on the history of philosophy created by it also collapses—*historia*.

\*

## The Essential Stubbornness of Metaphysics

Hegel calls everyday opining abstract thinking. He contrasts it with philosophy. In this way, however, he only shows, against his knowledge, that this opining is of *not only metaphysical* provenance, grounded upon metaphysics, but rather *represents metaphysics in its stubbornness*—in such a way that this opining, as if of its own accord, is in *possession* of everything (essential, pertaining to the essence) that for the thinking of beyng must be something *to be appropriated*.

Yet why this? Why not the unruffled indifference of what is public in the manner of the everyday?

\*

The essence *to* being capable of god—that of Dasein as ground of "*historicality*."

Taking over history.

## For X. The Owned

### Appropriative Event and the Owned

How the event of appropriation recedes into itself in the manner of an abyssal ground and in a concealed way bequeaths to its owned the entire gentleness of bestowal and all severity of struggle.

*

In what way the god?
 In need of beyng.
 Pointing back takes beyng *away* and thereby lets it come to its essence as the in-between.
 This event appropriates the reticence of his silence.

*

The human being and *sounding articulation*.
 The latter for *keeping reticent*—
 out of originary reticence.

*

Owned.
 The being of beings, specifically the *non-human*, determined and attuned from out of beyng.
 The exception of the *human* as taken out and steadfast insisting of Da-*sein*.
 Being in relation to beings no longer beingness, but rather essentially *historical* from out of the opening of appropriation.
 The gods and beyng?

*

World—uniquely apportioned into solitudes.
 Earth—retractively returning in a concealed manner in closure that preserves.

## For XI. The Configuration of Saying

Truth of beyng is the clearing of self-concealing.

Within it refusal essentially prevails, self-clearing refusal is the beckoning of beyng. Beckoning, beyng gathers itself into the bestowal of itself as singular.

No corresponding to beings is capable of bringing it to language. Say beyng.

## For XIII. Beyng-historical Thinking

*The remote*—from commencement to commencement.

As "seeing"—θεωρία—was determined by presencing, so beyng as event now demands *the word and hearing*. But at the same time no more metaphysics or ἰδεῖν as νοεῖν or the latter as *ratio*—but rather the truth of beyng essencing as the in-between in relation to all beings.

"Hearing"—not as another "sense," but rather following the *opening of appropriation,* a finding that awaits the coming—i.e., an awaiting finding of history.

Additional Materials for Κοινόν.
Out of the History of Beyng (1939–40)


*Power and Race*

"Race" is a power-concept—presupposes *subjectivity;* cf. on Ernst Jünger.[1] That is to say: only where the being of beings prevails in essence as power, albeit in a veiled and uncomprehended way, does the thought of "race" attain currency. It is inculcated into the consciousness of a people as an element of self-assertion, and indeed in connection with an emphasis on "biological" representation in general, especially when "life" has already been predetermined as a "struggle for existence." (Cf. the great esteem for Darwin in contemporary Russian communism.)

Conversely, where representation in terms of races and reckoning with racial forces arises, this must be regarded as a sign that the pure essence of power pertaining to being has been unleashed by being itself into being's abandonment of beings. This, however, characterizes the epoch of the consummation of metaphysics. The cultivation of race is a necessary measure to which the end of modernity is driven. To it there corresponds the harnessing of "culture," already prefigured in the essence of "culture," into a "politics of culture" that itself remains only a means of empowering power.

\*

Consummate meaninglessness: *being's abandonment.*
Κοινόν as the constitution of beings abandoned by being.
Yet here still being! Surely and indeed how!
Values—powerlessness—makeability—domain of making: *power.*
Not comprehended and grounded as being, however—rather the *full extension of power's essence* into the unconditional.
Full extension not simply "finding before us"—but rather first bringing to the powering of power.
This the Κοινόν.
Yet how historiographically.

---

1. Cf. *On Ernst Jünger, "The Worker."* Gesamtausgabe vol. 90.

# Editor's Epilogue

The two treatises *The History of Beyng (1938–40)* and Κοινόν. *Out of the History of Beyng (1939–40)* from Heidegger's literary estate appear here for the first time as volume 69 of the Complete Edition.

The manuscript of the treatise *The History of Beyng* comprises two major parts. At the beginning of the first main part of the manuscript we find the title "The History of Beyng = I"; and at the beginning of the second we find "The History of Beyng. I. Continuation = II." These two parts are divided into 13 subordinate parts and 178 sections. Since no table of contents has been provided, either by Heidegger himself or by his brother Fritz, the numbering of the superordinate titles in Roman numerals and of the subordinate sections in Arabic numerals comes from the editor. This sectioning not only suggests itself formally but is also justified by the proximity of the volume in terms of content to the *Contributions to Philosophy (Of the Event)*, which already displays this manner of sectioning the text.

The manuscript of the first part of the treatise *The History of Beyng* consists of 288 consecutively numbered pages in DIN A 5 format or occasionally in a smaller format. Pages 224 through 288 are notes that Heidegger probably added to the manuscript as preliminary work for the treatise proper. A few of these notes have been reproduced in the Appendix. The manuscript of the second part of this treatise consists of 95 consecutively numbered pages in a page format corresponding to that of the first part. In both parts of the manuscript, the continuous numbering is located on the lower left or right of each page. On the top right, Heidegger recorded an internal section numbering with numerals and letters.

The manuscript of the short treatise "Κοινόν. Out of the History of Beyng," written in the year 1939–40, comprises 23 pages consecutively numbered on the top left. Evidently Heidegger extensively altered the beginning of this treatise, since on the page numbered 3 on the upper left, on which half of what was written has been crossed out, the number 9 appears on the top right.

The "Draft for Κοινόν. On the History of Beyng," which must by no means be regarded simply as a preliminary version of the first text with slight variations, but must rather be regarded as an independent treatise in its own right, consists of 10 typewritten and 2 handwritten, unnumbered pages that show significant revisions and insertions on the part of the thinker. No manuscript exists of the typewritten text.

The transcript of the first part of the treatise *The History of Beyng*, which like that of the second part was done by Fritz Heidegger, is set out on 87 pages consecutively numbered on the top right. Pages 52a through 52w are specially numbered. Six handwritten pages are inserted into page 48. The transcript of the second part comprises 37 pages consecutively numbered on the top right.

The second treatise edited here, "Κοινόν. Out of the History of Beyng," has been transcribed onto 18 pages by Fritz Heidegger. From the second page on, there appear two series of numerals on the upper right, since one typewritten page contains more than just one page of the manuscript. The pages display several of Heidegger's marginal remarks. To the transcript there are attached handwritten "Additional Materials for *Κοινόν*," which appear in the Appendix.

The editor transcribed all those parts of the manuscript for the main text that had not yet been converted to typescript. Of the notes that served Heidegger as preliminary work for *The History of Beyng*, only those that are taken up into the Appendix were transcribed. The handwritten supplements in the manuscript and transcript that Heidegger drew attention to through insertion marks were incorporated into the running text. Marginal remarks that could not be inserted appear as footnotes.

Here two different kinds of footnotes are employed. Arabic numerals serve to record references internal or external to the text. Lowercase letters designate marginal remarks in the manuscript or transcript. To indicate where the particular marginal comment is found, the abbreviations Ms. for Manuscript and Trs. for Transcript are used.

Those volumes of the Complete Edition cited bibliographically that give no indication of year of publication have not yet appeared at the time of the publication of the present volume.

The typewritten transcripts were repeatedly compared to the manuscripts. The editor provided titles for a few sections where Heidegger did not give a title. The sections in question are 16, 51, 92, 138, 151, 152, 155, and 157. Occasional misreadings by his brother, which Heidegger overlooked when comparing the transcript with the manuscript, have been corrected. Clear slips of the pen have been quietly rectified. Abbreviations were expanded where possible. The punctuation was checked and supplemented or corrected where necessary. Underlines, which in the brother's transcript are indicated by extra spacing, appear in italics in the printed edition, as is the norm for volumes of the Complete Edition.

The two treatises *The History of Beyng (1938–40)* and *Κοινόν. Out of the History of Beyng (1939–40)*, as well as the treatise *The Overcoming of Metaphysics* (1938–39) from the same period, stand in a substantive relation to the *Contributions to Philosophy (Of the Event)*, which in turn bears a coherent connection to other major treatises of that period that are developed in terms of the history of beyng, such as *Mindfulness* (1938–39).

Like the *Contributions to Philosophy*, *The History of Beyng* experiences and thinks the "truth of beyng" as "event." With a view to the "event" from the perspective of the history of beyng, there also arises the question concerning the "overcoming of metaphysics." This overcoming, in which the appropriate language for beyng-historical thinking must first be found, necessitates a confrontation with the historical phenomena of modernity's consummating itself in the "power" of "machination." The extent to which the *Contributions to Philosophy*, again admittedly only as a "preliminary work," remain binding for such a confrontation is indicated by a page on which Heidegger records the plan for a "Sequence of Publications (in short treatises)." For the treatise *The History of Beyng*, as for the matter itself, the "draft of the *Contributions*" is to be retained "as its innermost structure."

In the treatise "Κοινόν. Out of the History of Beyng," the task of interpreting the historical actuality of metaphysically constituted modernity from out of the history of beyng sets itself to work. The war that began in September of 1939, and that Heidegger thinks as a beyng-historical phenomenon, leaves behind its trace. The center of the treatise, however, is the relationship between "machination" and "power," a relationship that attains its consummation in the shape of "communism." "Communism," however, is here by no means to be understood as the title of an ideology but is the concept for a particular structuring of beings as a whole that comes to appear at the end of the history of metaphysics. The "Draft for Κοινόν. On the History of Beyng" fundamentally discusses the same questions as the first treatise, but in its details focuses on other aspects of the topic. The "Draft" concludes differently from "Κοινόν," however, with words concerning the "coming of the last god."

*

I thank the administrator of the literary estate, Herr Dr. Hermann Heidegger, for the trust placed in me through the task of editing this volume and for his checking of portions of the manuscript deciphered by me. I thank Herr Prof. Dr. Friedrich-Wilhelm von Herrmann, who supported me in a truly helpful manner regarding all questions of editing. My thanks are due to Herr Prof. Dr. Heinrich Hüni, with whom I discussed in particular issues of deciphering, but also and through repeated readings the matter itself, which is not external to the work of editing. Thanks is due also to Herr Dr. Hartmut Tietjen for careful assistance with deciphering. Finally, I thank Herr cand. phil. Frank Schlegel and Frau Anne Untermann for their work in comparing and correcting.

Wuppertal, Fall 1997                                              Peter Trawny

# German–English Glossary

| | |
|---|---|
| das Abendland | Western world |
| abendländisch | Western, belonging to the Western world |
| der Abgrund | abyss |
| der Ab-grund | abyssal ground |
| ahnen | to intimate |
| die Ahnung | intimation |
| der Anfang | commencement |
| anfangend | inceptive |
| anfänglich | inceptual, pertaining to commencement |
| Anfänglichkeit | inceptuality |
| der Anklang | resonance |
| die Anwesung | presencing |
| die Armut | poverty |
| der Aufgang | emergence |
| der Auftrag | mandate |
| der Augenblick | moment |
| die Auseinandersetzung | critical encounter, discussion |
| die Auseinander-setzung | critical setting apart |
| die Aus-einander-setzung | offsetting from one another |
| der Austrag | sustainment |
| der Aus-trag | sustainment, carrying out of |
| austragen | to sustain |
| die Austragsamkeit | ability to be sustained |
| der Befehl | command |
| die Befreiung | freeing |
| der Beginn | beginning |
| der Begriff | concept |
| die Begründung | founding |
| beherrschen | to dominate |
| die Beherrschung | rule, domination |
| die Bemächtigung | power, assumption of |
| die Berechenbarkeit | calculability |
| die Bereitschaft | readiness |
| die Besinnung | reflection |
| die Be-sinnung | reflection on sense |
| die Beständigkeit | persistence, constancy |
| der Bezug | relation |
| die Botmäßigkeit | subjection |

das Christentum	Christendom

das Da	the There
die Diktatur	dictatorship
der Drang	urge, drive, impetus
die Durchmachtung	powering through

eigentlich	authentic
das Eigentum	the owned, property
das Eigentümliche	the peculiarly own
einfach	simple
die Einfachheit	simplicity
die Einförmigkeit	uniformity
einmalig	unique
sich einrichten	to install, institute itself
die Einrichtung	installation, institution
der Einsatz	intervention
einzig	singular
die Einzigkeit	singularity
die Endlichkeit	finitude
die Enteignung	disappropriation
die Ent-eignung	dis-appropriation, dis-appropriating
die Entgegnung	countering
die Ent-gegnung	en-countering
entlassen	to release
die Entmachtung	disempowering
die Ent-rückung	rapturous removal or transport
die Entscheidung	decision
das Entsetzen	horror
entwerfen	to project
der Entwurf	projection
das Erdenken	creative thinking
sich ereignen	to happen as event
sich er-eignen	to appropriate itself
das Ereignis	appropriative event, event
das Er-eignis	event of appropriation
die Ereignung	appropriative event, the happening of appropriation, the opening of appropriation

die Er-eignung	opening of appropriation
ergründen	to fathom the ground
die Ergründung	fathoming the ground
die Erinnerung	recollection
ermächtigen	to empower
die Ermächtigung	empowering
das Erscheinen	appearing
das Erschrecken	terror

# German–English Glossary

| | |
|---|---|
| erschüttern | to disrupt, shatter |
| die Erschütterung | disruption, shattering |
| er-stimmt | opened and attuned |
| ertragen | to withstand |
| die Erwesung | essential prevailing, bringing about of |
| die Er-wesung | opening up the essencing or essential prevailing |
| | |
| fügen | to enjoin |
| | |
| der Gang | passage |
| das Gefüge | configuration |
| die Gegnerschaft | opposition |
| die Gegnis | counterance |
| das Gemächte | that which is contrived, contrivance |
| die Geschichte | history |
| geschichtlich | historical |
| die Geschichtlichkeit | historicality, historicity |
| das Geschick | destining |
| das Geschlecht | generation |
| die Gewährung | granting |
| die Gewalt | violence |
| die Gewalttat | violence, act of |
| die Gewalttätigkeit | violence, violent activity |
| die Gewesenheit | having-been |
| die Ge-wesenheit, die Ge-wesung | having-been, essential |
| das Gewöhnliche | the habitual |
| das Gewohnte | the customary, habitual |
| die Gewöhnung | habituation |
| die Geworfenheit | thrownness |
| das Gleiche | the same |
| die Gleichförmigkeit | homogeneity |
| die Gleichgültigkeit | indifference |
| die Gleichmachung | equalization |
| der Gott | the god |
| die Gottschaft | godship |
| der Grimm | wrath |
| die Großmut | magnanimity |
| der Grund | ground |
| die Grundstimmung | attunement, fundamental |
| die Gründung | grounding |
| | |
| die Haltung | stance |
| der Herr | master, sovereign, lord |
| die Herrlichkeit | glory |

| | |
|---|---|
| die Herrschaft | dominance, sovereignty, rule, dominion |
| herrschen | to control, to rule |
| die Historie | historiography |
| | |
| der Inbegriff | concept, comprehensive |
| das Innestehen | standing within |
| die Innigkeit | intimacy |
| die Inständigen | those who steadfastly insist |
| die Inständigkeit | steadfast insistence |
| die In-ständigkeit | steadfast in-sistence |
| inständlich | instantiated |
| das Inzwischen | the in-between |
| die Irre | errancy |
| | |
| die Jähe | suddenness |
| | |
| der Kampf | struggle |
| der Knecht | slave, servant |
| die Knechtschaft | slavery, servitude |
| die Kraft | force, strength |
| | |
| die Langmut | forbearance |
| lichten | to clear |
| die Lichtung | clearing |
| loslassen | to unleash, relinquish |
| die Loslassung | unleashing |
| | |
| die Machbarkeit | makeability |
| die Mache | making, domain of |
| die Machenschaft | machination |
| die Machsamkeit | malleability |
| die Macht | power |
| machten | to power, wreak power |
| die Machtentfaltung | power, implementation of |
| der Machthaber | power, possessor of |
| die Machthaberschaft | power, possession of, institution of |
| mächtig | powerful |
| die Mächtigkeit | powerfulness |
| die Machtmehrung | power, increase in |
| der Machtträger | power, bearer of |
| die Machtverteilung | power, distribution of |
| die Maßnahme | measure |
| das Menschentum | humankind |
| | |
| die Neuzeit | modernity |
| nichtig | nihilative |

| | |
|---|---|
| das Nichtige | the nihilative |
| das Nichts | the nothing |
| die Nivellierung | leveling-down |
| die Not | need |
| die Not-losigkeit | need-lessness |
| das Notwendige | the necessary |
| | |
| das Offene | the open, open realm |
| die Ohnmacht | impotence |
| | |
| die Rasse | race |
| der Raum | space |
| rechnen | to calculate |
| das Rechnen | calculation |
| das Reichtum | wealth |
| das Riesige | the gigantic |
| das Russentum | the Russian world |
| | |
| die Sachlichkeit | matter-of-factness |
| die Sage | saga |
| säumen | to default |
| der Schein | semblance, illusion |
| das Scheinen | shining, shining semblance |
| schweigen | silent, to keep |
| der Schwung | arc |
| das Seiende | a being, beings, that which is |
| das Seiende im Ganzen | beings as a whole |
| die Seiendheit | beingness |
| das Sein | being |
| die Seinsvergessenheit | oblivion or forgottenness of being |
| die Seinsverlassenheit | being's abandonment |
| das Selbe | the Same |
| das Seltsame | the strange |
| die Sendung | mission |
| das Seyende | beyngs |
| das Seyn | beyng |
| seynsgeschichtlich | beyng-historical |
| der Sinn | meaning, sense |
| die Sinnlosigkeit | meaninglessness |
| die Sorge | care |
| der Sprung | leap |
| die Spur | trace |
| die Stätte | site |
| die Stille | stillness, silence |
| stimmen | to attune |
| die Stimmung | attunement |
| der Streit | strife |

| | |
|---|---|
| die Subjektität | subjectity |
| die Subjektivität | subjectivity |
| | |
| die Technik | technicity |
| die Temporalität | Temporality |
| tragen | to bear, carry, lend support |
| der Trieb | drive |
| | |
| übereignen | to appropriate over |
| die Über-eignung | being appropriated over |
| der Übergang | transition, passage over |
| übermachten | to overpower |
| die Übermächtigung | overpowering |
| die Überwindung | overcoming |
| uneigentlich | inauthentic |
| die Ungeschichte | history, corrupted |
| das Ungewöhnliche | the inhabitual |
| der Ungrund | non-ground |
| die Unruhe | restlessness, unease |
| die Unterscheidung | distinguishing, distinction |
| der Unterschied | distinction |
| die Unterwerfung | subjugation |
| das Unversehentliche | the unexpected |
| das Unwesen | essence, corrupted |
| | |
| die Verarmung | impoverishment |
| verbergen | to conceal |
| verborgen | concealed |
| die Verborgenheit | concealment |
| das Verbrechen | crime |
| die Vergegenständlichung | objectification |
| das Verhältnis | relationship |
| die Verknechtung | enslavement |
| verlassen | to abandon |
| vernichten | to annihilate |
| die Verrechnung | accounts, settling of |
| das Versäumnis | default |
| die Verschenkung | bestowal |
| die Verschleierung | veiling |
| verschließen | to close off |
| verwahren | to preserve |
| die Verwahrung | preservation |
| die Verweigerung | refusal |
| die Verwindung | recovery |
| die Verwüstung | devastation |
| verzwingen | to coerce, impel |

German–English Glossary

| | |
|---|---|
| das Volk | the people |
| das Volkstum | folklore, national tradition |
| die Vollendung | consummation |
| vollständig | complete |
| die Vollständigkeit | completeness |
| vorausdenken | to think ahead |
| voraustragen | to support in advance |
| vorbeiziehen | to pass by |
| das Vorbeiziehen | passing by |
| vordenken | to thoughtfully anticipate |
| die Vorläufigkeit | precursiveness |
| die Vormacht | power, dominant or supreme |
| der Vorrang | priority, precedence |
| das Vorstellen | representation |
| das Vor-stellen | representational setting-before |
| das Vorweg-denken | thinking, anticipatory |
| | |
| walten | to hold sway |
| die Weile | the while |
| werfen | to throw |
| die Wertung | valuing |
| wesen | essence, to prevail in |
| das Wesen | essence, essential prevailing |
| die Wesung | essencing, prevailing of the essence, essential prevailing |
| | |
| die Widerlegung | refutation |
| der Widerspruch | contradiction |
| der Wider-spruch | contra-diction |
| die Wiederholung | repetition |
| die Wieder-Holung | retrieval, fetching back |
| der Wieder-spruch | re-iteration |
| der Wink | beckoning |
| wirken | to effect |
| wirklich | actual, real |
| die Wirklichkeit | actuality, reality |
| die Wirksamkeit | effectiveness |
| die Würde | worthiness, dignity |
| die Würdigung | honoring |
| der Wurf | the throw |
| die Würfel | the dice |
| die Wüste | wasteland |
| | |
| zaudern | to vacillate |
| die Zeit | time |
| die Zeitlichkeit | temporality |
| der Zeit-Raum | time-space |

| | |
|---|---|
| der Zeit-Spiel-Raum | time-play-space |
| das Zerbrechen | shattering |
| der Zerfall | disintegration |
| die Zerstörung | destruction |
| zögern | to hesitate |
| die Zu-eignung | appropriating, coming to be appropriated |
| die Zugehörigkeit | belonging |
| die Zukunft | future |
| die Zu-kunft | the "to come" |
| die Zuweisung | assignment |
| der Zwang | force, compulsion |
| die Zwietracht | conflict |
| zwingen | to compel, force |

# English–German Glossary

to abandon — verlassen
abandonment, being's — die Seinsverlassenheit
ability to be sustained — die Austragsamkeit
abyss — der Abgrund
abyssal ground — der Ab-grund
accounts, settling of — die Verrechnung
actual, real — wirklich
actuality, reality — die Wirklichkeit
to annihilate — vernichten
appearing — das Erscheinen
to appropriate itself — sich er-eignen
to appropriate over — übereignen
appropriated, coming to be — die Zu-eignung
being appropriated over — die Über-eignung
appropriation, event of — das Er-eignis
appropriation, opening of — die Er-eignung
appropriative event — die Ereignung
arc — der Schwung
assignment — die Zuweisung
to attune — stimmen
attunement — die Stimmung
attunement, fundamental — die Grundstimmung
authentic — eigentlich

to bear, carry, lend support — tragen
beckoning — der Wink
beginning — der Beginn
being — das Sein
a being, beings, that which is — das Seiende
beingness — die Seiendheit
beings as a whole — das Seiende im Ganzen
belonging — die Zugehörigkeit
bestowal — die Verschenkung
beyng — das Seyn
beyng-historical — seynsgeschichtlich
beyngs — das Seyende

calculability — die Berechenbarkeit
to calculate — rechnen
calculation — das Rechnen
care — die Sorge
Christendom — das Christentum

## English–German Glossary

| | |
|---|---|
| to clear | lichten |
| clearing | die Lichtung |
| to close off | verschließen |
| to coerce, impel | verzwingen |
| the "to come" | die Zu-kunft |
| command | der Befehl |
| commencement | der Anfang |
| to compel, force | zwingen |
| complete | vollständig |
| completeness | die Vollständigkeit |
| to conceal | verbergen |
| concealed | verborgen |
| concealment | die Verborgenheit |
| concept | der Begriff |
| concept, comprehensive | der Inbegriff |
| configuration | das Gefüge |
| conflict | die Zwietracht |
| consummation | die Vollendung |
| contradiction | der Widerspruch |
| contra-diction | der Wider-spruch |
| contrivance, that which is contrived | das Gemächte |
| to control, to rule | herrschen |
| counterance | die Gegnis |
| countering | die Entgegnung |
| creative thinking | das Erdenken |
| crime | das Verbrechen |
| critical encounter, discussion | die Auseinandersetzung |
| critical setting apart | die Auseinander-setzung |
| the customary, habitual | das Gewohnte |
| | |
| decision | die Entscheidung |
| default | das Versäumnis |
| to default | säumen |
| destining | das Geschick |
| destruction | die Zerstörung |
| devastation | die Verwüstung |
| dice | die Würfel |
| dictatorship | die Diktatur |
| disappropriation | die Enteignung |
| dis-appropriation, dis-appropriating | die Ent-eignung |
| disempowering | die Entmachtung |
| disintegration | der Zerfall |
| to disrupt, shatter | erschüttern |
| disruption, shattering | die Erschütterung |
| distinction | der Unterschied |
| distinguishing, distinction | die Unterscheidung |

English–German Glossary 203

| | |
|---|---|
| to dominate | beherrschen |
| drive | der Trieb |
| | |
| to effect | wirken |
| effectiveness | die Wirksamkeit |
| emergence | der Aufgang |
| to empower | ermächtigen |
| empowering | die Ermächtigung |
| en-countering | die Ent-gegnung |
| to enjoin | fügen |
| enslavement | die Verknechtung |
| equalization | die Gleichmachung |
| errancy | die Irre |
| essence, corrupted | das Unwesen |
| essence, essential prevailing | das Wesen |
| essence, to prevail in | wesen |
| essencing, prevailing of the essence, essential prevailing | die Wesung |
| essential prevailing, bringing about of | die Erwesung |
| event | das Ereignis |
| event of appropriation | das Er-eignis |
| | |
| to fathom the ground | ergründen |
| fathoming the ground | die Ergründung |
| finitude | die Endlichkeit |
| folklore, national tradition | das Volkstum |
| forbearance | die Langmut |
| force, compulsion | der Zwang |
| force, strength | die Kraft |
| founding | die Begründung |
| freeing | die Befreiung |
| future | die Zukunft |
| | |
| generation | das Geschlecht |
| the gigantic | das Riesige |
| glory | die Herrlichkeit |
| the god | der Gott |
| godship | die Gottschaft |
| granting | die Gewährung |
| ground | der Grund |
| grounding | die Gründung |
| | |
| the habitual | das Gewöhnliche |
| habituation | die Gewöhnung |
| the happening of appropriation, eventful happening | die Ereignung |

| | |
|---|---|
| having-been | die Gewesenheit |
| having-been, essential | die Ge-wesenheit, die Ge-wesung |
| to hesitate | zögern |
| historical | geschichtlich |
| historicality, historicity | die Geschichtlichkeit |
| historiography | die Historie |
| history | die Geschichte |
| history, corrupted | die Ungeschichte |
| to hold sway | walten |
| homogeneity | die Gleichförmigkeit |
| honoring | die Würdigung |
| horror | das Entsetzen |
| humankind | das Menschentum |
| | |
| impotence | die Ohnmacht |
| impoverishment | die Verarmung |
| inauthentic | uneigentlich |
| the in-between | das Inzwischen |
| inceptive | anfangend |
| inceptual, pertaining to the commencement | anfänglich |
| inceptuality | Anfänglichkeit |
| indifference | die Gleichgültigkeit |
| the inhabitual | das Ungewöhnliche |
| to install, institute itself | sich einrichten |
| installation, institution | die Einrichtung |
| instantiated | inständlich |
| intervention | der Einsatz |
| intimacy | die Innigkeit |
| to intimate | ahnen |
| intimation | die Ahnung |
| | |
| leap | der Sprung |
| leveling-down | die Nivellierung |
| | |
| machination | die Machenschaft |
| magnanimity | die Großmut |
| makeability | die Machbarkeit |
| making, domain of | die Mache |
| malleability | die Machsamkeit |
| mandate | der Auftrag |
| master, sovereign, lord | der Herr |
| matter-of-factness | die Sachlichkeit |
| meaning, sense | der Sinn |
| meaninglessness | die Sinnlosigkeit |
| measure | die Maßnahme |

## English–German Glossary

| | |
|---|---|
| mission | die Sendung |
| modernity | die Neuzeit |
| moment | der Augenblick |
| | |
| the necessary | das Notwendige |
| need | die Not |
| need-lessness | die Not-losigkeit |
| nihilative | nichtig |
| the nihilative | das Nichtige |
| non-ground | der Ungrund |
| the nothing | das Nichts |
| | |
| objectification | die Vergegenständlichung |
| oblivion or forgottenness of being | die Seinsvergessenheit |
| offsetting from one another | die Aus-einander-setzung |
| the open, open realm | das Offene |
| opened and attuned | er-stimmt |
| the opening of appropriation | die Er-eignung |
| opening up the essencing or essential prevailing | die Er-wesung |
| opposition | die Gegnerschaft |
| overcoming | die Überwindung |
| to overpower | übermachten |
| overpowering | die Übermächtigung |
| the owned, property | das Eigentum |
| | |
| passage | der Gang |
| to pass by | vorbeiziehen |
| passing by | das Vorbeiziehen |
| the peculiarly own | das Eigentümliche |
| the people | das Volk |
| persistence, constancy | die Beständigkeit |
| poverty | die Armut |
| power | die Macht |
| power, assumption of | die Bemächtigung |
| power, bearer of | der Machtträger |
| power, distribution of | die Machtverteilung |
| power, dominant or supreme | die Vormacht |
| power, implementation of | die Machtentfaltung |
| power, increase in | die Machtmehrung |
| power, possession or institution of | die Machthaberschaft |
| power, possessor of | der Machthaber |
| to power, wreak power | machten |
| powerful | mächtig |
| powerfulness | die Mächtigkeit |
| powering through | die Durchmachtung |
| precursiveness | die Vorläufigkeit |

| | |
|---|---|
| presencing | die Anwesung |
| preservation | die Verwahrung |
| to preserve | verwahren |
| priority, precedence | der Vorrang |
| to project | entwerfen |
| projection | der Entwurf |
| | |
| race | die Rasse |
| rapturous removal or transport | die Ent-rückung |
| readiness | die Bereitschaft |
| recollection | die Erinnerung |
| recovery | die Verwindung |
| reflection | die Besinnung |
| reflection on sense | die Be-sinnung |
| refusal | die Verweigerung |
| refutation | die Widerlegung |
| re-iteration | der Wieder-spruch |
| relation | der Bezug |
| relationship | das Verhältnis |
| to release | entlassen |
| repetition | die Wiederholung |
| representation | das Vorstellen |
| representational setting-before | das Vor-stellen |
| resonance | der Anklang |
| restlessness, unease | die Unruhe |
| retrieval, fetching back | die Wieder-Holung |
| rule, domination | die Beherrschung |
| the Russian world | das Russentum |
| | |
| saga | die Sage |
| the same | das Gleiche |
| the Same | das Selbe |
| semblance, illusion | der Schein |
| shattering | das Zerbrechen |
| shining, shining semblance | das Scheinen |
| silent, to keep | schweigen |
| simple | einfach |
| simplicity | die Einfachheit |
| singular | einzig |
| singularity | die Einzigkeit |
| site | die Stätte |
| slave, servant | der Knecht |
| slavery, servitude | die Knechtschaft |
| sovereign, master, lord | der Herr |
| sovereignty, rule, dominion | die Herrschaft |
| space | der Raum |

# English–German Glossary

| | |
|---|---|
| stance | die Haltung |
| standing within | das Innestehen |
| steadfast insistence | die Inständigkeit |
| steadfast in-sistence | die In-ständigkeit |
| stillness, silence | die Stille |
| the strange | das Seltsame |
| strife | der Streit |
| struggle | der Kampf |
| subjection | die Botmäßigkeit |
| subjectity | die Subjektität |
| subjectivity | die Subjektivität |
| subjugation | die Unterwerfung |
| suddenness | die Jähe |
| to support in advance | voraustragen |
| supremacy, dominant power | die Vormacht |
| to sustain | austragen |
| sustainment | der Austrag |
| sustainment, carrying out of | der Aus-trag |
| | |
| technicity | die Technik |
| temporality | die Zeitlichkeit |
| Temporality | die Temporalität |
| terror | das Erschrecken |
| the There | das Da |
| to think ahead | vorausdenken |
| thinking, anticipatory | das Vorweg-denken |
| to thoughtfully anticipate | vordenken |
| the throw | der Wurf |
| to throw | werfen |
| thrownness | die Geworfenheit |
| time | die Zeit |
| time-play-space | der Zeit-Spiel-Raum |
| time-space | der Zeit-Raum |
| trace | die Spur |
| transition, passage over | der Übergang |
| | |
| the unexpected | das Unversehentliche |
| uniformity | die Einförmigkeit |
| unique | einmalig |
| to unleash, relinquish | loslassen |
| unleashing | die Loslassung |
| urge, drive, impetus | der Drang |
| | |
| to vacillate | zaudern |
| valuing | die Wertung |
| veiling | die Verschleierung |

| | |
|---|---|
| violence | die Gewalt |
| violence, act of | die Gewalttat |
| violent activity | die Gewalttätigkeit |
| | |
| wasteland | die Wüste |
| wealth | das Reichtum |
| Western, belonging to the Western world | abendländisch |
| Western world | das Abendland |
| the while | die Weile |
| to withstand | ertragen |
| worthiness, dignity | die Würde |
| wrath | der Grimm |

Lightning Source UK Ltd.
Milton Keynes UK
UKHW010217310720
367471UK00004B/522

9 780253 018144